The Barefoot Veterinarian

Other books available from All Publishing Company:
www.allpublishingcompany.com

Pot-Bellied Pet Pigs, Mini-Pig Care and Training
by Kayla Mull and Lorrie Blackburn, D.V.M.

Veterinary Care of Pot-Bellied Pet Pigs
by Lorrie Boldrick, D.V.M.
(a.k.a. Lorrie Blackburn, D.V.M.)

Pygmy Goats: Management and Veterinary Care
by Lorrie Boldrick, D.V.M.

Front cover artwork by John Rehak

The Barefoot Veterinarian

"Tails" of a Semi-Rural Orange County
Veterinarian

by
Lorrie Boldrick, D.V.M.
with
Michael Boldrick, Ph.D.

All Publishing Company
Orange, CA 92865
2008

Published by:

        All Publishing Company
        2387 N. Flanders St.
        Orange, CA 92865
        www.allpublishingcompany.com

Library of Congress Control Number: 2008907164

ISBN: 978-0-9624531-4-4

Dedication

To all my patients and their owners – who helped make my veterinary career fun, memorable, and always educational (that is why it is called the "practice" of veterinary medicine).

Lorrie Boldrick

To Bashan.

Michael Boldrick

Table of Contents

Acknowledgments

Thanks to:

My little brother, Mikey, who has often been a bratty little brother, but *always* a special friend. Who would have thought that he was a creative writer? Originally, this book was to be written by me "as told to" Mikey. But since he is so familiar with many of the stories, he was able to add much information that I had not remembered or included. So I upgraded him to co-author.

My little sister, Jane, the first person to encourage me to write this book. She did an excellent job of editing. She dotted the i's, crossed the t's, and more importantly, caught and corrected inconsistencies and repeated information repetition. Perhaps most significantly, the title of the book (and some of the stories) was her idea.

My other brother, Johnny. He reviewed the first draft and surprised me, not because he could read, but by reading the entire book, actually liking the stories and encouraging us to proceed.

Lydia Hale, my co-author of *Pygmy Goats, Management and Veterinary Care*, who also reviewed the first draft. She found a few minor mistakes, but she was very positive and encouraging. She did want to know what baby boa constrictors eat when they are newborns. I didn't find a place to put it in the book - so, Lydia, they eat baby mice.

Karen Keb Acevedo, who is an editor by profession and a published author. She read the "almost final" draft and, happily, didn't tell me I should stick to veterinary medicine (i.e., not give up my day job). She had helpful ideas and corrections but was overall extremely positive in her appraisal.

Kathy Loveless and Nan Keder, who also read the late draft and offered insightful suggestions (even though I didn't like or incorporate some of them).

Last, but not least, the Quillie Acres Veterinary Clinic staff and other friends who put up with me talking about this for the past ten years. It has finally come to fruition!

Introduction

Some vets are known for their surgical prowess; others for their uncanny ability to diagnose unusual cases. Expertise in caring for exotic animals – in the heart of Southern California, no less – also gains one recognition. While I like to think I enjoy a good reputation for my surgical and diagnostic skills, and I'm quite confident of my reputation for treating a vast array of exotic breeds, it seems that my most memorable characteristic lies elsewhere … in my feet, to be precise. I have always worked barefoot.

I can list several practical reasons to not wear shoes but I recognize there are at least an equal number supporting the need for footwear. It really comes down to this: I'm most comfortable when I'm barefoot and I'm the boss, so I can get away with it. After over thirty years (or should that be "almost forty years") of practice, working barefoot is as much a part of me as is my love for animals and my desire to provide them with the best care I possibly can.

I always enjoy the surprised, perplexed or sometimes dismayed look on a new client's face when he or she notices my lack of shoes. I was recently reminded that many of my clients identify me by my bare feet when a long-time client accompanied his friend that was visiting my clinic for the first time. Just as I stepped into the exam room to greet them and their pet, the new client looked at his friend and exclaimed, "You were right! She's not wearing any shoes!"

The Barefoot Veterinarian

I am not completely inflexible (although, please don't ask my staff to confirm this) as I have made exceptions and worn shoes when the situation warranted. These occasions include the brief times that I worked at other clinics and when I've done not-so-brief contract work for American Wilderness Zoo and Aquarium, Disneyland, Knott's Berry Farm, Orange County Zoo and Santa Ana Zoo, all of whom required that I wear shoes when I worked on their properties.

That's the story behind the title of this book, but the fact that I was usually shoeless was not the only unique part of my career. Much more interesting is that I got to treat a lot of animals some vets never even lay eyes on, let alone take care of. The zoos and parks provided me the opportunity to work on deer, turtles, tortoises (up to 400 pounds!), monkeys, and many species of bird. Not your typical small-animal practice, but still fairly mundane. I also regularly ministered to snakes, sloths, seals, bats, lemurs, rock hyraxes, dik-diks, and even mountain lions and dolphins. This is still just the beginning of the list of species that I treated, which also includes goats, sheep, pigs, llamas, wallabies, and ferrets that were kept as pets by my clients. Yes, Orange County, the grand suburb of Los Angeles it is thought to be, is still blessed with a surprising amount of open land, at least along its periphery, providing ample space for all these animals one would not normally associate with the city.

And we can't leave out my own personal menagerie, as I acquired, or had foisted upon me, many exotic animals as pets of my own. Now that I no longer live in my home of twenty-five years and am down to two dogs and one cat, I can safely admit - without fear of animal control sweeping in to arrest me - that the highest my personal pet count reached was seventy-eight, all on one and a quarter acres in the hills of Orange County.

This book is a collection of the memorable experiences this varied assortment of animals provided throughout my career. Although presented in roughly chronological order, each story can stand alone. While there are some recurring characters - mostly family members, pets and staff - you won't be lost if you choose to hop around reading select stories. Not all the stories are about exotic animals, as I did treat many dogs and cats and they are actually the "stars" of some of the most unusual incidents in the book.

Out of respect for the privacy of my clients and patients, I have changed their names. I have also taken literary license to expand and enhance many of the stories, but the core experiences are all genuine. I expect, and hope, that some readers will recognize themselves, their pets or friends. I apologize if you are disappointed that your real name isn't in print or if you don't like the pseudonym I have given you. And, please, excuse any liberties I've taken with the facts. I have also kept references to the zoos and parks generic. While I don't consider any of the stories to be critical or even marginally incriminating, I also don't believe they in any way hinge on the identity of a specific location.

Some of the stories will make you smile, many will make you laugh, others will make you sad and a few may even make you cry. Hopefully, they'll all make it clear what an extraordinarily rewarding and often entertaining career I've had caring for animals - and often their owners!

Beginnings

The Start of a Book

In 1972 James Herriot wrote a book called All Creatures Great and Small, a fantastic story of his life as a veterinarian. I make no claim to be the caliber of writer of Mr. Herriot, but I do have some fun and interesting stories to tell. And one, while not the first in chronological order, is very similar to the first story in his book, so let's start there.

I earned my veterinary degree (D.V.M.) from the University of California, Davis in ... well, let's just say before Mr. Herriot published his book. I moved from Davis to Southern California and began my career assisting at two small-animal clinics in Orange County. I also occasionally covered for another veterinarian who specialized in goats and sheep. While working these three jobs, I married Tom, and a couple of years later, in June 1974, our first child, Allie, was born. Her birth served as the impetus for me to strike out on my own, as I wanted to spend more time being "just a mom."

One of the first cases for my practice was a house call, which predictably came on an unusually rainy, windy and generally miserable August night, a little after ten. A goat had been attacked by a pack of neighborhood dogs and injured badly – severely enough that his owners, Anne and Bill Rodgers, were afraid to load him into their truck for the forty-five-minute drive to my clinic. Rather than have me go on the house call alone, my husband Tom said he and two-month-old Allie would come along to keep me company.

Shiloh, my patient, was a large, statuesque Alpine wether, dark brown with three white stockings, white around his nose and both eyes and a white behind. He was in shock, so his brown eyes seemed overly large, yet unfocused. Both of Shiloh's back legs had been chewed extensively, exposing flesh and muscle all the way up to his hips. He couldn't stand up, but the damage did not appear irreparable. Anne and Bill had already laid him on a blue-plastic tarp in a vacant horse stall, providing me with a relatively clean environment and plenty of room to treat poor Shiloh. Anne sat beside him, petting and comforting him, trying to keep him still. Bill helped me fetch my instruments from the van and then joined Anne in restraining Shiloh as I assessed the damage. After my initial examination, I gave Shiloh an injection of antibiotics and began the long process of cleaning and suturing wounds.

While I was busy working on Shiloh, Tom waited just outside the stall, observing and holding a fast-asleep Allie. The neighbor who had heard the commotion and chased off the dogs attacking Shiloh also kept a close eye on the proceedings. He reminded me of an old cowboy, his plaid-shirted forearms resting on the top rail and one muddy boot propped up on the bottom rail. With his straw cowboy hat tipped back and a piece of hay in the corner of his mouth, he chatted away in a surprisingly deep southern drawl. Although I was focused on the goat, I couldn't help but overhear a few of his remarks, catching things like, "Back in Arkansas we would have hung him in a sling." And, "Back in

Arkansas Doc Wilson would have flushed the wounds with turpentine."

After nearly two hours of steady work, I finished all I could do that night and made arrangements to come back the next day to check on Shiloh. As we were driving home, Tom commented, "That call was just like the first chapter of All Creatures Great and Small." We had both recently read the book and in the first chapter, while the young veterinarian is struggling to deliver a calf, an old farmer sits in the back of the barn maintaining a constant commentary of how his vet, Mr. Broomfield, would have done everything differently and certainly would have pulled the calf and finished already. Perhaps the Rodgers' neighbor had read the book, too?

The erstwhile "expert" neighbor was never there for any of my follow-up visits, but I assume he was as pleased with Shiloh's progress as everyone else. And I am happy to report that after six weeks of nursing and physical therapy by his owners Shiloh recovered very nicely and my private practice was off to a successful start.

Veterinary School

Laying Down on the Job

I knew I wanted to be a vet when I was five years old. I don't really know what led to that decision. I don't even remember making it, but my folks enjoyed telling of how one evening at dinner when asked what I learned at kindergarten that day, I replied, "I'm going to be a veterinarian." At the time they were so impressed that I knew and could pronounce the word "veterinarian," they paid little attention to the statement itself or that it wasn't really an answer to their question. Perhaps I had gotten in trouble at school and was trying to change the subject - I was rather precocious - or maybe I had an epiphany. While other careers, nurse and horse trainer among them, were at one time or another appealing, my choice never truly wavered. I don't have any regrets, but if I had known some of the issues that would come up, I might have reconsidered. You see, I am and always have been deathly afraid of needles; I have a freakishly low tolerance for pain; and I faint at the sight of human blood. You might begin to question why I was attracted to medicine, but I had no worries. After all the needles weren't meant for me, pain shouldn't be involved, and I didn't intend to perform surgery on humans. You're probably familiar with the saying that starts "The best laid plans ..." Well, mine went awry very quickly.

My first semester of vet school, I took a physiology class that included a laboratory section where we got to work on live animals. I was psyched! This was what I had been waiting for since that day in kindergarten. After several weeks of lectures, our first day actually working with live animals finally arrived. You could feel the nervous energy vibrating through the entire laboratory, and I was certainly contributing more than my fair share. My first patient was Heinz, a ten-year-old Dachshund. I don't, however, remember what procedure we were learning that day. This might seem strange considering Heinz was my very first patient - ever. But perhaps it's because I have such a vivid memory of the events that transpired before any actual surgical procedures were begun.

In the lab, we worked in teams of three. Team members rotated between the positions of surgeon, assistant and anesthesiologist. My role that day was anesthesiologist. Carefully following the steps described by Professor Higgins in lecture and then demonstrated by Dr. Clement in the lab, I loaded a syringe with the anesthetic. I surprised myself by getting the needle in Heinz's vein on the first try and aspirated a small amount of blood into the syringe to verify that I was indeed in the vein. So far, so good. Then, as the blood filtered back into the syringe, I passed out and collapsed on the floor. I was out cold. And although I wasn't out long, it was long enough to earn a visit to the Student Health Center to be checked out. One of the teaching assistants escorted me to the Health Center while the remainder of my team tended to Heinz. I remember being told he recovered wonderfully from his anesthesia, but I still don't recall what procedures I was to have learned that day. Either I learned them later or I've never needed them in the many years since. Physically, I, too, recovered quickly, but you can only imagine the teasing I took from my fellow classmates!

Sadly, as you'll read throughout the book, this would not be the last time I passed out on the job.

Dangerous Effects of Rabies

I actually managed to stay on my feet until my third year of vet school. I had secured a great job at the Department of Animal Resources caring for many of the animals used by the school. I was thrilled to finally be earning money for working with animals. That is until about a month into the job when the department decided that all employees had to get a prophylactic rabies vaccine. Remember that list of things I'm not too fond of, as in scared to death of? Remember what was at the top of the list? Yeah, that's right. Needles. I generally avoid them at all cost, but I liked the job and I really needed the money.

So, I joined the entire Department of Animal Resources in traipsing across campus to the Student Health Center. This was the late 1960s, so I expected passersby to start walking with us, assuming we were leading some sort of protest march. In my head, I was protesting vociferously the idea of getting this shot. I trailed along at the back of the group with the vain hope that they'd run out of serum before it was my turn. No such luck.

When it was my turn, I hesitantly sat in the sterile-looking, white plastic chair and stretched out my arm. I immediately started feeling warm. My temperature continued rising as the nurse rolled up my sleeve, and I was literally sweating by the time she swabbed my arm with alcohol (which did nothing to relieve the heat I was feeling). The prick of the needle piercing my skin was the end; I fainted.

The nurses were terrific. They gave me orange juice and lots of TLC. Everyone else went back to work, but I had to stay at the Health Center until the nurses were assured I had completely recovered. Fortunately, nobody at Animal Resources had been in my first-year physiology class so they weren't aware of my history of fainting. I was teased of course, but only mildly.

Parents do the Craziest Things

It goes without saying that vet students must love animals. The job pays well, but if you're in it just for the money, there are plenty more lucrative professions to choose from. I certainly proved my commitment to the animal kingdom by allowing myself, albeit accidentally, to be anesthetized in place of Heinz, the Dachshund. Many other students displayed their passion in a more traditional way - by having pets. Some of their pets, however, were far from traditional. My classmates had an armful of oddities – referring, at least for the moment, to the pets, not the students.

On the not-too-strange end of the scale was Kevin Gentry, whose folks gave him a six-foot-long boa constrictor snake. I only thought this a little odd but had to laugh when I learned the story behind Rex. Kevin originally received him as a gift for his fifteenth birthday but left Rex in his parents' care when he headed off to college, as the dorms had a strict no-pets policy. Rex was well cared for by Kevin's parents, albeit not quite as lovingly, throughout Kevin's undergraduate years. Mrs. Gentry was immensely proud of her son when he was accepted to vet school. She was almost equally excited that he was moving to an apartment. Apparently she hadn't been exactly thrilled when her husband initially gave their son a snake, and after spending four years feeding poor little white mice to Rex, she could stand it no more. Rex was leaving her house. So Kevin was given his pet snake - for a second time!

Those of you with kids can probably relate to the experience of being stuck with their abandoned pets. It starts with their first puppy. They promise they'll walk, feed and clean up after Fido, and do so ... for three days. The pattern repeats until they head off to college leaving you with one last forgotten pet. Kudos to Mrs. Gentry for pushing back.

I hadn't had much exposure to snakes, but I thought Rex was pretty cool. I absolutely, positively can not say the same for my friend Jay's pet, which he received as a "got into vet school" present. It still makes me squirm uncontrollably to even think about it. His parents should have been arrested for child endangerment! I can't believe any self-respecting mother would participate in such a gift! What kind of critter could raise my ire to such a fever pitch? A tarantula. Yuck! Yuck! Double yuck! I failed to mention them earlier, but add spiders to the top of that list of things I am deathly afraid of. Fortunately I heard about Terry the tarantula through the grapevine and was therefore able to steadfastly avoid going in Jay's room. For that matter, I avoided going anywhere near his apartment.

Hey, I couldn't be certain the little monster hadn't escaped and was waiting patiently to pounce on me as I passed by.

Pets Gone Wild

Speaking of pouncing reminds me of probably the most unique human-animal relationship I have ever come across. It wasn't during vet school, but years later in the mid 1970s. Laurie Marker worked as a veterinary technician at a wild animal park in the Northwest. I met her when she was in Southern California to attend a conference on big cats (as in lions, tigers, cheetahs, etc.). Although I worked on cats myself, they were decidedly smaller varieties (Tabbies, Siamese, Calicos, etc.), so I wasn't even aware of the conference. It was Georgianna, a mutual friend, that suggested I might be willing to host Laurie for the week. We hit it off marvelously, and I made more than one trip up north to stay at her place at the wild animal park.

I admit I went to visit Laurie for more than her terrific company. For starters there was the special access to all the magnificent animals at the wildlife park, which was fabulous, but it was more than that. You see, Laurie was one of those people who was always bringing work home with her. A briefcase full of paperwork is one thing, but for Laurie it was a young cheetah. Khayam had to be taken away from her mother as a very young cub, and Laurie got the task of bottle feeding and generally hand raising her. Because such a young cub requires frequent feeding, Laurie received permission to take Khayam home with her. They formed a unique, intense bond, and Khayam continued to go home with Laurie for over nine years. Instead of setting up a cheetah-sized litter box, she taught Khayam to use the shower to relieve herself. That made cleanup easy for Laurie. And, yes, she used a different bathroom for her own hygienic needs.

Lorrie doing her version of the circus trick "stick your head in the mouth of a lion." Actually, it was what Laurie Marker called a cheetah kiss.

Their unprecedented relationship led to a first-of-its-kind of research project. Laurie and Khayam flew to Namibia, Africa to see if a captive-bred cheetah could be taught to hunt in the wild. After months of sitting patiently at waterholes being taught the steps of hunting by her adopted "mother," Khayam took down her first antelope. Laurie never did manage to catch one herself. Laurie and Khayam became celebrities, touring the country telling the cheetah's story until Khayam's death in 1986.

Laurie's passion for cheetahs did not die with Khayam. While in Africa, she learned that a cheetah's survival depended not only on being able to hunt, but also on being able to avoid Namibian farmers, who were killing hundreds of wild cheetahs each year to allegedly protect their livestock. Dr. Laurie Marker (she received her doctorate from Oxford University in 2003) continued to travel to Africa regularly until 1990 when she founded the Cheetah Conservation Fund, housed in Namibia. The CCF has grown into a renowned research and education facility, with one of its primary focuses being to teach farmers that they can safely share the land with cheetahs.

Monkeying Around

Perhaps the parents of veterinary school students had a secret communication method (this was long before email), or maybe it was because my parents had heard enough of my stories about the snake, tarantula and other unique pets at school. But it turns out I wasn't to be left out of the odd pets contingent. It was Christmas vacation of my second year of vet school and I made the two hour drive from Davis to my folks' home in Santa Cruz. It was a warm December day, so I made the trip with the top down on my 1958 VW bug. I made the trip in record time, pulling up in front of the house well before my promised noon arrival. I was greeted by a note taped to the front door ordering me to wait outside until my mother returned from visiting friends. I had a key and I was anxious to get in and use the bathroom, but I found the note peculiar enough to obey.

Fortunately, Mom wasn't long and pulled in the driveway within ten minutes. She was very relieved to see that I was waiting outside. After a quick hug and a little catching up on the front porch, I pleaded with her to go inside so I could use the facilities. She explained that my Christmas present was not wrapped and required a bit of explanation. After I made my required stop, she led me to the back of the house. Somewhat bewildered, I followed her into the master bathroom. There, in a small cage, was a very young Capuchin monkey! She was dark brown with light brown arms and shoulders and a flesh-colored mask with dark brown around her eyes, nose and mouth. Mom said that she and Dad thought she was the perfect Christmas present for me. They were probably right. I was shocked, thrilled, taken aback, amazed, dazed, confused and tickled pink – all at once. If that sounds like a weird case of emotional overload, it was!

Mom said they had purchased the monkey, whom I named Kippy, two days earlier from a specialty pet store thirty miles away in San Jose. We had always had at least one dog as I was growing up so my folks had plenty of experience with pets, but a monkey was definitely something new for them. Mom was a clean freak – her house was always spotless – so I think her love of our pets was always tempered by the mess they created, although it probably wasn't all that much added on top of what four kids and a husband generated. When I considered all this and that she let a monkey live in her bathroom for two days, I was amazed and deeply touched. When I learned the rest of the story, I was even more shocked. I was actually surprised that my gift survived until I got there.

As I just mentioned, a monkey is not an ordinary pet, and Mom and Dad got a lesson on that point the first evening with Kippy. Dad opened the cage to put fresh water in her bowl and got schooled on how quick and slippery monkeys are as she slipped past his arm, out the cage door and loose into the house. At this point, the cage was not in the bathroom, but on the kitchen table, with the intention of letting my kid brother and sister enjoy her until Christmas. It would also keep Kippy from feeling isolated and help socialize her.

Once loose, Kippy immediately got in the Christmas spirit as she dashed across the kitchen counters instinctively seeking refuge in the nearest tree, which just happened to be the fully decorated Christmas tree. As Dad chased after her, Kippy took a flying leap up onto the tree. It wasn't rooted to the ground like the trees her ancestors had swung in, so the monkey, the tree, the lights and all the decorations went noisily crashing to the ground. While Mom screamed, the kids shrieked and the dog barked, Dad took advantage of the confusion and snatched up Kippy and returned her to her cage, which was subsequently moved to the back bathroom. This way, if she were to escape again, at least she would be contained. When I saw my dad's hand and arm two evenings later, I became less certain as to who had caught whom. His hands and lower arms were covered with bite wounds and scratches. Apparently, Kippy had put up quite a fight going back into the cage. By the time I arrived, Dad's wounds were the only evidence of the mishap. The Christmas tree was back up and redecorated with new, unbroken ornaments, and happily, my new monkey remained in one piece, albeit banished to the back bathroom.

Kippy was a delightful monkey, but she never forgave my father for his part in thwarting her escape. Whenever he came within her view, she would grin – and this was not a happy grin – and screech at him, rattling her cage viciously. If she was out of her cage, she would lunge at him. In spite of these hostile greetings and having been attacked and bitten, Dad really wanted to be friends with her. He genuinely loved animals, and it hurt him to be so loathed.

Kippy didn't always hate Dad, especially not when Dad allowed her to fish ice cubes out of his drink.

At home in my trailer, I let Kippy run free most of the time, but I had also trained her on a leash attached to a belt around her waist so I could take her out and about with me. I always used the leash when introducing her to someone new, even inside the trailer, just in case. It seemed that my dad was the only human she had it in for, but after seeing what she had done to him, I wasn't taking any chances.

Kippy was very bright, as are most monkeys, and loved to play games. One of her favorites was "catch." I, or whoever was playing with her, would roll a tennis ball to her. She would catch it and roll it back. The first time I bounced, rather than rolled the ball, she got scared and jumped higher than the ball bounced. She figured it out almost immediately, however, and became good at catching the bounced ball - even bouncing it back.

During one of my parents' visits the following summer, I wanted to show off Kippy's game-playing skills and figured it would be a good chance to let Dad try to make friends with her, so I put her on her leash and gave Dad a tennis ball to roll to her. She would throw/roll the ball back to him and they actually did engage in a game of "catch." At that time, Kippy was better at catch than my little brother, so both Dad and the monkey seemed to be having fun. But while she was playing games with him, Kippy was also trying to play games with me. She was slowly gathering up the slack in her leash with her tail and coiling it up behind her. In concert with this, she was rolling the ball a shorter distance each time she returned it, drawing my dad a little closer. You can imagine the trap she was baiting.

Since I noticed her collecting the leash, I was carefully pulling back on it to eliminate the extra coils she was accumulating. When she finally thought she had Dad suckered in close enough, she leapt at him but was very surprised and dismayed when all the leash she had collected had gone missing, leaving her short of her intended target. Luckily she didn't seem to realize that

I was the one who foiled her plan. At least she remained lovable and playful with me, as opposed to trying to maim me as she repeatedly did my father.

Follow Like Sheep

My job with the Department of Animal Resources - the one that required me to get a rabies shot, after which I passed out - was as an animal caretaker. The Department provided housing and care for all the animals that were available for or actively being used in research. "Animal Caretaker" was just a fancy title for "one in charge of feeding and watering animals and mucking their stalls." Many of the research animals housed by the Department of Animal Resources were part of long-term behavioral observations, so we got to know most of them quite well.

Among the collection were Fred and Barney, two adult male aoudads that lived in a thirty-foot long by six-foot wide covered pen. I know what you're thinking. "Wow! Amazing! Aoudads! I can't believe Lorrie really got to work with such exotic animals!" Followed by, "Hmmm? What the heck is an aoudad, anyway?"

Well, let me tell you a little about them. Auodads come from North Africa and they are quite rare even there. They are tan-colored members of the subfamily Caprinae (goat-antelope). If you saw one, you might mistake it for a bighorn sheep. Perhaps that's why these animals are also known as Barbary sheep. "So, you mean aoudads are just a type of sheep? What a letdown!"

While they are indeed sheep-like animals, aoudads exhibit the agility of a mountain goat and are quite shy. Barney and Fred were no exception, as both were quite timid around people and tried to stay as far away from us as possible when we went in to clean their pen, feed and water them. The gate opened near one end, along the long side of the pen, and when we entered, Barney and Fred would herd to the opposite end. As we worked toward them, they would pace nervously until they could stand it no longer and then "the boys" would race by us, often going so far as to bank up off the wall as they rushed past.

One day, Bert, a new employee - it's always the new guy or gal, isn't it - was responsible for the aoudads. They dutifully herded to the opposite end as Bert entered. We had warned Bert about how the boys would frantically race past him as he moved toward them and that he should give them as wide a berth as possible. Maybe they were alarmed by the new guy, but Fred and Barney went blasting by Bert before he was even half way down the pen. Bert quickly scaled the pen wall to get out of their way, inadvertently causing the pen door to fly open (he had failed to latched it properly - a definite no no). Barney skidded out through the opening, quickly followed by the ever-alert Fred. A few of us were nearby, monitoring the new guy, but no one was quick enough to capture either of the aoudads.

The Animal Resources facility was about a mile from the main U.C. Davis campus but it was on the other side of the highway. We got a demonstration of just how nimble aoudads are when Barney effortlessly bounded over the six-foot chain link fence that surrounded the facility. Fred was not quite so smooth. As he tried to leap over the fence, he somehow got his head caught between the chain link and the top bar. Since we were already giving chase, we quickly released him from his self-induced head-lock. He was uninjured - except maybe his pride at not having made it over the fence - and was quickly escorted back to the facility.

Barney, however, proved to be as agile mentally as he was physically; he ran along the train track that led under the highway to campus, thus avoiding any undoubtedly deadly encounters with traffic. He followed the tracks all the way into the main campus. We were in hot pursuit, although admittedly losing ground, and were just close enough to see him run through an open door into the Home Economics building. We may have been foolish enough to let him escape, but when we finally reached the door we saw him go through, we followed - and slammed the door behind us. He was out of sight, having already moved beyond the main hallway, but when we reached the tee, we saw him. Fortunately, he had turned right rather than left, as the corridor to the left led to glass doors, and there's no telling what might have happened if he had run toward an apparent opening. The four of us formed a wall and gently cornered him, grabbed hold and harnessed him. We led him safely back across campus, through the tunnel and into his pen. The aoudads got lots of extra exercise that day – and so did we! We also put a new twist on the phrase "follow like sheep."

Kippy Goes to the Dentist

When she was about six months old, I was cuddling Kippy and casually examining her at the same time. Monkeys commonly groom one another, so she was very comfortable with this. As I was looking inside her mouth, I noticed a cavity in one of her lower teeth. It didn't seem to bother her, but she was young and it was large, so I thought it should be treated.

However, there were no veterinary dental specialists back in those days, so I called my own dentist and asked for his help. Dr. Kirk was concerned about his qualifications to work on a monkey – such small teeth in such a small mouth – but his curiosity and the novelty of it all led him to agree. Kippy and I went to his office late on a Saturday afternoon, after all his patients were gone. We figured that while some of his clients might get a kick out of having a monkey in the waiting room, it might not be good for business if they thought they were sharing instruments with a Capuchin.

Judy, a good friend who loved and was loved by Kippy, came with us. She sat in the chair and held Kippy. She was sort of a human chair within the dentist's chair, using her arms as Kippy's seat belt. I gave her, Kippy that is, an anesthetic so she would relax and keep her mouth open for Dr. Kirk, with the not inconsequential benefit that she wouldn't bite him. I didn't tell him about how she attacked my dad, so he didn't know how worried he should be.

He carefully drilled out the cavity to remove all the surrounding decay, just as he would with a human patient, and put in a silver filling. Remember, this was along time ago, so all the marvelous, quick-set filling materials weren't available. As he tamped in the silver, he worried that he would hurt her jaw, but I supported it from underneath, and the whole procedure went very well. I only allowed her soft food that night, and it was like nothing had happened by the next day. Everything was going well until six months later, when the tooth fell out. I hadn't thought about it at the time, but it turns out that monkeys have baby teeth, just like their primate cousins, humans! I never did tell Dr. Kirk that he had worked so hard on a baby tooth.

I Got the Point

Veterinary medicine is not only about caring for animals while they are alive. It is important and sometimes critical to learn what we can from an animal that has died. Thus, our last year of vet school included a pathology lab. Only one month before graduation, my assignment for the day was to necropsy a two-month-old foal that had died from a very unusual joint infection. I was properly if not fashionably dressed in my coveralls, rubber boots and thick rubber necropsy gloves. I made my first incision into the foal starting in the middle of his abdomen and extended it up toward his head. I held the head extended with my left hand, and as I carried the incision forward I drove the point of the knife directly into the palm of my hand.

It took me a minute to realize what had happened. It didn't hurt right away, but I did feel something warm and sticky on my hand. As soon as I realized what I done and that it was my own blood rapidly filling my glove, I promptly fainted. While again entertained by my fainting, my classmates were good enough to rush me to the doctor.

In what was by then a semi-conscious state, my colleagues carried me into the waiting room at the Student Health Center. I remember hearing, "Hey, it's that vet student who faints. She's back again." The jovial kidding tones quickly gave way to more serious attention once the doctors and nurses realized that all the blood in the glove was actually mine. They quickly got the bleeding under control but remained quite concerned that I might contract whatever infection the foal I was working on had died from. As the only blood sample I had collected was my own and not from the foal, one of my classmates finished the necropsy I had barely started. It was a slightly nerve-wracking several days while we waited for the results of the cultures on the foal. It turned out that the foal had a viral infection that fortunately was not transmissible to humans. My stab wound healed without incident – except for the fact that it became yet another chapter in the legendary tales of the fainting vet!

Kippy Moves On

In my last year of vet school, I was so busy that I was hardly ever at home. After about a month I realized how unfair it was to Kippy to be stuck in a cage, alone almost all the time. About that time, the Shneiders invited me over for dinner. As a busy student, any home cooked meal was greatly appreciated, so I jumped at the opportunity. Teri was an administrator at the vet school, and she and her husband Glen had taken pity on me and fed me many times. They had three young sons, so the invitation was contingent on me bringing Kippy.

During the meal, I lamented how I was spending so little time with the poor monkey. We had a great meal, as usual, and the boys had a blast playing with Kippy. I was surprised the next evening when I received a call from Teri. Although she invited me over for dinner a couple times a semester, we didn't really have a "chatting" type of relationship. I was floored when she said the family had discussed it and would like to adopt Kippy for the rest of the school year. After some soul searching on my part, I agreed with the condition that this would be a permanent move. It was hard, but we agreed it would be best for Kippy not to bounce between homes. Plus I didn't know where I would be living the next year and expected I would be working long hours at my first real job. As much as I desperately missed her, I knew Kippy got a good deal.

Filling a Void

I took a rare vacation during my last year of vet school. During school breaks, I usually either worked (I was, after all, a nearly starving student), went to visit my folks in Santa Cruz (sometimes finding time to sneak down to the beach), or just hung out in Davis. Mostly, I just worked. Anticipating that vacation time would be hard to come by once I started a real job, I jumped at the chance to go camping with a few girlfriends during spring break. We were having unseasonably warm weather in early April, making sleeping outdoors sound almost fun. It also helped that camping is not very expensive.

Early Saturday morning, I left Sport, my two-year-old collie mix, with my good friends Pete and Doris, piled in the truck with the girls and headed to the Sierras. I thought I was being extremely adventurous. I was never a girl who always needed electricity for her hair dryer, but neither was I a forest ranger's dream woman. We drove about three hours to the trailhead and hiked a few miles through a gorgeous redwood forest that opened up to a stunning alpine lake at the base of the tallest peak in the area.

Jenny was the outdoorswoman of the group, so she pretty much set up both tents as the rest of us pretended to help. We did lend a hand collecting firewood that she turned into a terrific fire, which we sat around until late that night. Mostly, we reminisced about our soon to be completed veterinary training and our soon to start professional careers, but we might have snuck in a little discussion about men. Great hikes, relaxing by the lake and a quick dip in the freezing cold lake made for an awesome four days. Sadly, my memory of that trip is tinged with sadness.

The girls dropped me off around five Wednesday afternoon, so I immediately hopped in my truck and headed over to Pete and Doris's to pick up Sport. I got a weird feeling when she wasn't out in the yard, barking to greet me, but I figured she'd earned a pass into the house. If only that had been the case. It turns out that a day after I left on my trip, Pete was out front playing fetch with Sport – Pete was throwing, Sport was fetching – when Sport spied a rabbit and took off in pursuit. The rabbit dashed back and forth in the yard then headed toward the road. Before Pete could do more than yell, Sport followed it into the street and was hit by a passing car. I didn't hold Pete responsible for even a second, but I was crushed. It's impossible to describe how much I hurt. It still hurts to think about it. I was a vet student. I loved all animals. We had dogs when I was a kid, but Sport was the first pet that was "mine." I drowned my sorrows with two beers, which is two more than I had had the entire previous year. Even if I had been fit to drive, I couldn't bear the thought of going home to an empty house, so I stayed with Pete and Doris.

As days passed, the pain dulled slightly, but I still didn't like having an empty house to come home to each evening. I wanted another dog. My father knew that even before I got Sport I had been dreaming of owning a Newfoundland. He also knew that I couldn't afford to buy one. He called less than a week after Sport's death and asked how much a Newfoundland would cost. Through tears of sadness, at having lost Sport and frustration at not being able to afford a new dog, I told him, "Two hundred dollars." That's not a drop in the bucket today, but it was a lot back then. Dad then said he had two hundred dollars that he wanted to invest in a Newfoundland but he didn't want to have to keep the dog at his house – would I keep it? What a nice way to give me the money for the dog. I'm sure you agree, I had a pretty special dad.

Even today, Newfoundlands aren't an overly common dog, so the search for my new companion began. After a disappointing week of searching the Davis and

Sacramento area, I got a call from Doris, who was visiting her mom in Southern California. She had located a litter of Newfoundland puppies and had already found out that there were still two puppies available. I flew down the next day and came home with an eight-week-old Newfie puppy who I named Osa, Spanish for "bear." As I think about it, I'm not sure how a starving student who couldn't afford a dog managed to buy a round-trip ticket to Southern California! But PSA and Air California were the predecessors of Southwest Airlines, today's low-cost airline, so I imagine the airfare was pretty cheap.

Thelma Erikson, a vivacious mother of two, pregnant with number three, was the breeder who sold me Osa. When I spoke with her before flying down, she stated she was only selling the pups to homes with small children, but that she would make an exception for me. I'm not sure what Doris had told her, but I didn't care. I was getting my Newfoundland! Thelma kept track of Osa for all thirteen years that I owned her, and I'm quite sure she never regretted her decision to let one pup go to a home with no children. It was easy for her to check on Osa for the first three months I lived in Southern California – where I got my first job – as I lived with the Eriksons in what would soon be the baby's room. Thelma is still my very dear friend.

Hooked on Fish

I will always remember my first case after finishing vet school. The last year of vet school seemed to go on for a very long time, and much of it was spent studying for State Boards. State Boards were critical because we had to pass them before we could get a license to practice veterinary medicine in California. No pressure, right? The exams took two full days in late May. And so what if we had to wait a very long two months before we were informed of the results (unlike the nearly instant results available today). After the stress of preparing for and finally taking them, there was a lot of relief at just having finished the Boards. I think every senior veterinary student left town immediately after the exams and headed for some rest and relaxation away from Davis. At that point, we were just glad they were over!

One of my best friends was Becky Jordan. Becky's grandparents had a quaint, white clapboard cottage on the beach just outside Santa Cruz. Better yet, her grandparents were out of town and said we could have the house for the weekend. Within an hour of finishing Boards, Becky and I loaded our bathing suits, beach towels, sunglasses, a couple of trashy romance novels and our two dogs into my black convertible VW bug and made the two-hour trek to Santa Cruz. We were mentally exhausted but also extremely excited to have the exam – and four years of vet school – behind us. We decided to start the next morning with a long walk along the beach with the dogs before plopping ourselves into beach chairs to relax and soak up the sun for the rest of the day.

The Barefoot Veterinarian

Osa, my young Newfoundland, and Josie, Becky's Border Terrier, were well-trained, so we let them off leash and began our stroll along the water's edge. It always made us laugh to watch two such size-mismatched dogs play so well together. Adding the ocean and its small waves washing in and out, which neither dog had ever seen, made it even more entertaining. As we were walking, rehashing the exam and laughing at the dogs, we almost stumbled into a pair of gulls – commonly called seagulls, but that is actually incorrect terminology – trying to fly, but unable to do so.

We put the dogs on a down-stay, approached calmly and cautiously and captured the birds. They had both tried to eat a fish that had already been caught on a fishing-line with multiple hooks. Now, the gulls were caught on the same hooks as the fish. I suppose if they could have moved in perfect coordination, they could have made it off the ground, but they kept trying to fly away from each other resulting in a Keystone Cops skit instead of a smooth getaway.

As conscientious veterinarians, Becky and I each removed the hook from our respective bird's beak. We carefully examined their beaks (and the rest of the gull) and decided that their wounds were not serious. We released them nearly simultaneously, and they flew away immediately. They never even looked back to say thanks! Becky and I, however, were still very proud of our Good Samaritan act. But we enjoyed the rest of the weekend without having to perform any more unlicensed veterinary procedures.

Private Practice

Now, That's Interesting

My first job after vet school was at Cypress Dog and Cat Hospital. Although the hospital was owned by head veterinarian Ian O'Hara, the de facto queen was Muff, a very mellow, medium-sized tabby. She was there when I started working for Dr. O'Hara and retained her "hospital cat" throne until she died at age twenty. Muff slept in a cage at night but had free run of the hospital during the day and she would strut around as if she really did own the place. The wood-paneled waiting room was a fifteen foot square with beige tile floor (easy to clean up "accidents"). The receptionist's desk was next to the door that led to the exam rooms and green-cushioned chairs lined the walls. Muff's favorite resting spot was the third chair from the desk. She considered it "her chair." If a client happened to be sitting there when she was ready to nap, Muff just jumped into the client's lap (even if it was already occupied by their pet!), curled up and went to sleep. Some clients would look at us like we should really do something, but we would just smile, shrug our shoulders and reply, "Sorry, that's Muff's chair." Of course, if she was already sleeping in her chair when the waiting room became crowded, she would never consider moving just so a client could sit down. I never did see anybody try to displace her. Perhaps it's better we never found out how she would have reacted.

In addition to being willing to share her chair – if the human got there first, Muff was also remarkably tolerant of the myriad events that happen in a veterinary hospital. Yowling cats and barking dogs were just part of life, never waking her or causing her any apparent distress. One day I was certain that her curiosity would be piqued. I had a young pig, Mu Shu Pork, come in for castration, and as we rarely saw pigs at Cypress, I expected Muff to at least show some interest. The pig squealed incessantly, as do all pigs when they are restrained, but Muff totally ignored it. It was almost lunchtime when I finished the procedure. I kept Mu Shu on the table so I could monitor him as he came out from under anesthesia. A staff member brought me my lunch - burgers and fries from a local fast food joint. As soon as she heard the bag rustle, Muff instantly appeared on the table, sitting on the pig's nose (seriously!), trying to see what we had brought for "her" lunch.

Somebody Call a Doctor

When I first graduated from veterinary school, I was very proud of being called "Doctor." As a child growing up, I was taught to address adults as Missis, Mister or as appropriate, Doctor. That was the way of the South, but the emphasis on the "Doctor" portion was likely influenced by my dad being an MD. I taught my children to show the same respect to their elders, and I remember emphasizing the proper use of Dr. too, no doubt because of my status as a DVM.

Not long after I started at Cypress Dog and Cat, Mom and Dad came down from Northern California to visit. I know my dad was relieved to have the first of four kids finally off the dole, but it was also parental instinct that compelled them to make sure their eldest child was safe in her new home and being treated well at her new job. My rental home was nothing special, but I was particularly excited, and a little bit nervous, to take them into work and show them around. As we were making our tour, Susan, one of the technicians and already a close friend, came up behind us and called, "Dr. Boldrick, may I speak to you?" I turned around only to see that Dad had also reacted to hearing "his" name. I'm sure he wouldn't have admitted it, but mixed in with his slightly confused and embarrassed look was a nod of proud approval. Susan didn't have anything important to ask me, she was just trying to impress my father with my new title. It worked!

It Runs in the Family

My medical ancestry was not limited to my father. My grandfather, John Tobin Boldrick, was a doctor who opened the first public hospital in Kentucky, and my grandmother was his nurse. My father, John Tobin Boldrick Jr, followed in his footsteps and became a general practitioner and general surgeon. Unlike me, Dad did not dream of a career in medicine; he always wanted to be a pilot. However, he gave in to family pressure and not only practiced medicine but excelled at it. He was respected by his colleagues and loved by his patients. His being pushed into medicine turned out to be to my benefit, as he encouraged me to pursue whatever career I desired.

Dad had a great sense of humor. He loved to pull your leg, and from stories I heard, so did his father. Dad usually wore sunglasses, so you couldn't see the gleam in his eye as he set you up, but his bright smile let you know it was all in fun when he "got ya."' He "got" me on the day I graduated from veterinary school at University of California, Davis. On graduation day, I started teasing him that I had more initials after my name (BS and DVM) than he did (MD). He proved degrees don't mean everything during the drive home when he nonchalantly asked, "Hey Lorrie, which type of cattle, Angus or Holstein, gives the best pork?" Being the anxious new doctor in the family, I didn't listen to the entire question and thinking he was asking about beef, fired back with, "Angus, of course." As the rest of the car burst out laughing, he quipped, "That's funny, I thought only pigs gave pork." Got ya!

Although Dad was a wonderful parent with a terrific sense of humor, he was not blessed with a strong heart. In the early 70s, while I was working at Cypress Dog and Cat Hospital, he suffered a major heart attack. He and Mom came to visit while he was recovering and not allowed to work. One Saturday morning, I went to work while he and Mom relaxed at my house. One of my patients that day was a ten-week-old light-tan Boxer puppy named Rocky who had been vomiting and not eating for the past week. I examined him and felt a mass in his abdomen that I thought was an intussusception. An intussusception occurs when the intestine telescopes into itself like a sock turned half way inside out, resulting in an obstruction. If my diagnosis was correct, surgery was the only way to fix this pup. Since the problem had been going on for at least a week, it was likely that I would not be able to simply "re-extend the telescope," but would have to surgically remove part of the intestine, an intestinal resection. Being a relatively young vet, I had never done such a procedure on my own, but I was the only vet on duty that day. I knew Dad did intestinal resections almost daily in his surgical practice, so I called my house and asked if he would be willing to come to the hospital and scrub in on this surgery with me. He had barely said, "Absolutely!" before he hung up the phone, and he must have broken several traffic laws to get to the hospital as quickly as he did. Obviously, he was no longer finding "relaxing" very relaxing, and was itching to get back to work, even if it wasn't on the species he was used to operating on. He performed his own brief examination, palpating Rocky's abdomen and disagreed with my diagnosis, but deferred to the trained veterinarian (me), and we proceeded with the surgery. I anesthetized Rocky and made my incision. I had barely opened the incision before you could see an obvious intussusception. My diagnosis was right! Boy, did that boost my ego. In spite of being shown up by his daughter, Dad talked me through an intestinal resection and I closed the incision, woke Rocky up and got him into a cage for recovery. He recovered marvelously.

Dad returned home to Santa Cruz the next week and went in for a checkup with his cardiologist. When he told him that he had assisted in surgery, the cardiologist was not impressed! He scolded Dad, reminded him that he was not on staff at any hospital in Southern California and furthermore he was supposed to be recovering from a heart attack and shouldn't have been doing surgery anyway. Dad sat back while the cardiologist completed his tirade. Then, grinning like the Cheshire cat, he explained that the patient was a Boxer pup. His cardiologist became speechless at that point.

Dad called me weekly to check on Rocky's recovery, just as he would any other patient. His calls also served another purpose ... to demand his assistant surgeon's fee! I didn't pay.

Looking back on that now, I still remember how excited I was to have made the right diagnosis when my father got it wrong. What has become perhaps more important with the passing of time (and sadly, of Dad) was the opportunity to interact professionally with my father.

Horsing Around

Bam was a Quarter Horse gelding I owned and loved for more than twenty years. I first met him soon after I started college at the University of California, Davis. Bam belonged to my roommate Doris, who kept him at a stable near school. He was just two years old, and Doris was training him to be a jumper, with visions of the two of them going to the Olympics in two years. Bam was terrific, but he and Doris didn't quite reach their aspirations of Olympic glory, finishing third in an event where they had to finish at least second to earn a berth in the Olympic trials.

Several years later, when Doris and I were both living in Southern California, I had the opportunity to buy

Bam. Doris, whose passion had shifted to dressage, bought a well-trained dressage horse and was looking for another home for Bam. I immediately offered to take Bam and the deal was made. Like many little girls, I had always loved to ride and dreamed of having my own horse. My dream had come true! Doris sold him to me for a song ($0.00 and the promise of a permanent, loving home), but if I had known what a special part of my family he would become, I would have paid a hundred times as much. Tough luck, Doris.

Bam was very smart as horses go. If a teenager got on to ride him and was not properly respectful, he would quickly buck that rider off. (I didn't have a problem with that, because I shared his attitude, sometimes wishing I could apply similar punishment to rude kids.) If a rider knew what he or she was doing, Bam was very well behaved. One day, I was leading him around the arena with three-year-old Erin on his back. As I was walking, Bam stopped quite suddenly. I turned around to scold him and tell him to get moving when I noticed that he was standing quite awkwardly, leaning way over to the right. Concern that he was injured immediately flashed though my mind, but then I noticed Erin was listing way over to the left, about to fall, but too stoic - or scared - to call for help. Bam was trying his best to tip his body so that she wouldn't topple off, and he knew that if he kept moving, she would surely end up on the ground. I straightened Erin in the saddle, praised Bam effusively and we finished our walk around the arena without further incident.

I love animals sometimes. OK, most of the time, but you know what I mean. The funny part is that Bam and I had nothing to really worry about. If Erin had fallen, even if she had been injured, her mom, Thelma, one of my best friends in the world, would have shrugged and said something like, "That'll teach her to hold on more tightly." Then again, Thelma would have harassed and embarrassed me about it for years, as she has done with the one or two other goofs I've made in her presence.

Bam taking Lorrie over a jump (both imagining Olympic glory).

Sarah Just Can't Let it Go

After a short time in Orange County living with my friends the Eriksons (the breeders of Osa, my Newfoundland) I found a house to rent and life settled down into a routine. A very busy routine. Osa was a spectacular companion, but I missed having a monkey. My little brother Mikey, who was nine years old at the time, was enough like a monkey to provide a good surrogate, but I only had him for a week during the summer (thankfully), so about a year and a half after I started my job, I bought a baby Spider monkey at a pet store in Santa Cruz. Yes, I went up to a pet store near my parents' house to buy Sarah, who was less than a year old, very recently weaned and weighed only four pounds. She was adorable and looked sweet and innocent. She was also very affectionate because she had already had lots of human contact. Kelly, the pet store owner, had spoon-fed Sarah for several weeks when she first arrived because she was in such poor condition. She was healthy when I got her, and I had no problem continuing to provide human contact in the form of hugging and petting.

Like many monkeys, including Kippy (a Capuchin), Spider monkeys have a prehensile tail, meaning they can grab with them, a bit like a hand. I'm sure you've seen monkeys using their tails as they swing in the trees. Pardon the momentary side trip to zoology class, but did you know that not all monkeys have a prehensile tail? Only some New World monkeys do. Old World monkeys, such as baboons and macaques, do not.

When I first got Sarah, she was so young that she hadn't mastered the use of her tail yet. It was a good thing she didn't weigh much, because as entertaining as it was to watch her learn, it could have been painful. You see, she was young and rather insecure, so whenever she was out of her cage, she would stand by me and wrap her tail around my wrist for security, sort of a monkey's version of a blankie I guess. Everything was fine until Osa walked by and Sarah decided to pounce on her. The problem was that she would forget to release her tail from my wrist. When she was rudely yanked back from her playful "attack," she would look at me like I had restrained her! Eventually she figured out how to let go with her tail too. Like any mother, while I was happy to see my little girl grow up, I was a little sad to have our "bond" broken.

Here, Let Me Help

Sarah may have attacked (albeit playfully) Osa initially, but it wasn't long before she traded in my arm for Osa as her security blanket. When I would take the two of them out for a walk, Sarah would ride on Osa's back like a little jockey. The shocked and surprised looks on passers-by were priceless. I especially loved the thrilled and amazed looks on small children. It was entertaining to observe how some people would engage me in conversation, while others would speak to and make noises at Sarah and Osa. Still others would wait until they passed and then comment among themselves. I couldn't always hear what they said, but often heard a lot of good laughs.

Sarah frequently climbed down to explore bushes, picket fences, sprinklers and her favorite – flowers. She was still pretty insecure, so if something startled her, she would scamper back and hop onto Osa's back. They were an odd couple – a big, black long-haired dog and a wiry, short-haired silver and black monkey – but they were the best of friends and spent many hours wrestling, playing and sometimes just resting together. It was just another of about a gazillion examples of what an awesome, gentle dog Osa was.

Their close friendship did cause a minor problem. Osa was about four years old and I discovered a small tumor on her side. I suspected it was a lipoma (a fatty tumor which is not cancerous), but it was the first I found on her, so I chose to remove it surgically. I took advantage of how calm Osa was and did the procedure with local anesthesia, so she never even missed a meal. Happily, the tumor was benign, as expected. She was a very cooperative patient and never licked or chewed at her incision. Sarah, on the other hand, was fascinated with the sutures. I let some clients remove stitches from their animal if I trust them to wait the requisite time and to confirm that the incision has healed well, but Sarah didn't seem prepared to conform to my rules. She started by lightly picking at the sutures, but soon seemed intent on removing them long before the wound was healed. I had to keep her separate from Osa for the entire healing period, causing them both a lot of distress. I did relent occasionally, but only when I was willing to sit with my hand over the incision. Sarah was somewhat mollified by being able to play and hang out with her buddy, but was frustrated when I would shoo her away from the stitches. Thank goodness it was only ten days before I removed the stitches, and they could get back to wrestling and playing.

The Dog on the Flying Trapeze

Osa was a very tolerant dog, even when she was very young. Whenever I went to visit my folks, their small poodles would constantly harass her. Peanut, a black teacup (i.e., very small) poodle, was a puppy at the same time as Osa. Mind you, Peanut weighed barely a pound soaking wet, and Osa was already tipping the scales at twenty-five pounds when they were both eight weeks old. At a year of age, Osa weighed one hundred pounds to Peanut's four pounds, but someone forgot to tell Peanut that he was small and should have some respect for much larger dogs. Can you say Napoleon complex? One of Peanut's favorite tricks was to jump up, grab onto Osa's ear and hang there, even while Osa shook her head in a half-hearted attempt to get rid of him. I thought Peanut was being a real pest - he was - and I was concerned he was hurting Osa's ear - he wasn't. Before I could step in and rescue Osa - I didn't worry that Peanut might lose his hold and slam into the wall - I realized that Osa was making no effort to avoid him when he started leaping after her droopy ears. If anything, she lowered her head slightly. It turns out they were very good buddies. I think Peanut just liked to "fly," and Osa enjoyed giving him the thrill.

Peanut and Osa, an odd couple, but very good friends. Peanut is laying between Osa's front paws - the fuzzy blob with a bow on his head.

What's in a Name?

Terminology has long been a problem in our society. We are unwilling to call "certain body parts" by their correct names. Oops, I guess now I'm guilty, too. Very early in my veterinary career, three teenage boys called with an emergency. It was a Sunday afternoon and the pet hospital was closed, and I was the on-call vet. The boys' dog, Max, had been lifting his leg on a bush and was now bleeding profusely. They could not – or would not – tell me exactly where the blood was coming from. All they would say was that he was bleeding "you know, down there." Up to that point, my experience with teenage boys was limited to when I was a teenage girl. Even that experience was limited considering I went to an all-girls boarding school. After a few probing questions failed to elicit any more specific description of the site of the injury, I told them I'd meet them at the hospital.

The three boys and Max were waiting for me when I arrived. James and John, tall and skinny, red-headed twins, were standing with their hands in their pockets and heads pointed down, peering up with only their eyes to shyly greet me. Luke, a muscular, black-haired, young man with a face full of acne, but a very engaging smile, was squatting next to Max, stroking him lovingly. Max was an eighty-pound male Labrador Retriever with a blocky head and a lush yellow-blonde coat. Glancing at his paws and belly, it looked as if he had splashed through a can of red paint. I unlocked the front door and ushered them into an exam room.

Although there was a lot of blood on his coat, the wound was not a "gusher," and Max was a very calm patient. He readily rolled over on his back – probably expecting a belly rub – so I could search for the source of the bleeding. I should have guessed it. The blood was coming from the opening in his penile sheath. That explained the boys' discomfort at describing the precise location of the bleeding. I extended the penis out the opening and found a two-inch cut along the side of the penis. It was easily sutured and would heal well. Proper recovery did present another challenge, however. Since the penis stays up in the sheath most of the time, it was likely that as the wound healed it would adhere to the inside wall of the sheath. Someone would have to manipulate the penis several times a day so it would not end up "stuck." When I sent the dog home the next day, I explained the situation to the boys. All three of their faces turned as red as James' and John's hair, but they said they would get the job done. I was adamant about the importance, but still skeptical that my instructions would be followed. Later in the week, I happened to see the boys at a fast food restaurant. Luke came up to me and said, "Hi Dr. Boldrick. Max is doing great and everything is working just fine." I'm not sure if his love for his dog overcame his extreme discomfort at his assigned task (and for the likely ribbing he got from his buddies), if Max manipulated "it" himself or if we were simply fortunate the penis didn't adhere to the inside of the sheath. No matter. Max was great and "everything" was working fine.

Go to the "Head" of the Line

Most of us are familiar with waiting lines at the grocery store, DMV (Department of Motor Vehicles), doctor's office and the hospital emergency room. They are at least annoying, sometimes aggravating and occasionally downright infuriating. Maybe the worst is when you've been waiting for what seems like hours and somebody walks in the door and seems to go right to the front of the line. What makes them so special? My twisted ankle really hurts! So what if they have blood pouring from a gunshot wound? They should know better than to try to stop a bullet with their body! Tongue in cheek aside, there are ways to "go to the head of the line" at my clinic and the Jensens found one of those ways with Roscoe.

Roscoe was their brand new eight-week-old Australian Shepherd puppy. He was a white and blue (actually a shade of gray that is called "blue" in Australian Shepherds) fuzzball of loving energy. Australian Shepherds have been bred as working dogs, so they are energetic to the point of being hyperactive. Add this bred-in energy to the energy typical of all puppies, and you can begin to get a picture, albeit a fast-moving, blurry one, of Roscoe. It was Roscoe's first day at his new home, a sunny Saturday, and the whole family – Steve, Kathy, the twins Ryan and Kevin, and little brother Griffin – was in the backyard playing. Roscoe would bound from one coaxing voice to the next, but with his short attention span, would then bolt off to investigate the bushes and anything else he could find in the yard.

When he disappeared behind the shrub and didn't reemerge when called, the kids went to see what had him so enraptured. Rather than being "enraptured," it turns out Roscoe was "captured" by an old glass gallon jug. It must have been used to store something that smelled very good because he somehow managed to squeeze his head all the way into the jug in pursuit of whatever prize he thought must be in there. The problem came when he wanted to get his head back out.

When the boys called him, he lifted his head, but the jug came with it. He pawed at it unsuccessfully, so he took off with his new headgear. If the situation were in a cartoon, it would have been funny to watch Roscoe running around with his head stuck in a gallon jug, but this was not a cartoon. Steve grabbed and held the puppy, but try as she might, Kathy could not pull the jug off his head. Roscoe quickly became restless and tried to wriggle out of Steve's grasp. He was panting heavily inside the jug. Concerned that he might not be getting enough air, Steve had one of the boys fetch a hammer and tried to break the jug to free the little guy's head. Partial success. The bell part of the jug broke nicely, and Roscoe could breathe freely, but the neck of the jug was still intact around his neck, so now he had many spikes of glass sticking out around his face.

They decided a trip to the vet was in order and very carefully carried him into my hospital. After my initial shock at seeing Roscoe in his current condition, I must admit I started laughing. The laughing didn't last long because Roscoe wasn't laughing. No one could even pet his head, because it was surrounded by spikes of glass. He didn't seem to understand why his new playmates were no longer willing to play with him. I took him into the back room, away from his family, which seemed to calm him slightly. With the help of two of my technicians, I was able to slowly work the skin back behind the neck of the jug and pull it off his head. What a happy puppy he was now that he could be cuddled and loved again! He was never in pain from the jug, but had been in definite emotional distress from being held at a distance from his new friends.

Choke Hold

Thus far, I've tried to avoid specifically dating myself, but I remember February 9, 1971. That was the day the Sylmar/Newhall earthquake struck. It was the first major earthquake to rock the area after I moved down to Southern California. I had experienced several substantial temblors while living in Northern California, but this one was a real doozy. The epicenter was forty miles from my rental house in Cypress, but it felt like Disneyland had just opened a new roller coaster right in my bedroom. At the unacceptably early hour of 5 a.m., I was awakened by the not-so-gentle shaking, rattling and rumbling of my house. It wasn't just the vicious motion, but also all the associated creaking, groaning and clanging noises. No, not generated by my body – I was still very young at the time – but by my house. Adding injury to the insult was all the plaster falling from the ceiling, in both chunks and a steady snow of chalk dust. I wasn't actually injured, but I was certainly insulted by the early wakeup call and the plaster rain, as was Osa, my two-year-old Newfoundland. She was clearly unnerved, wide-eyed and panting. About the time I figured out we were having a major earthquake, she jumped up on the bed looking to me for reassurance. She obviously didn't know who she was dealing with, as I was considering diving off and under the bed myself. Realizing I had to be the adult and comfort her, I started stroking her with one hand and telling her everything was OK. I wasn't convincing myself, and Osa didn't seem to buy it either. I only used one hand because with the other I was hugging her. Well, actually I was holding on to her for dear life and practically choking her in the process. Talk about your mixed messages!

Contrasting Osa's and my reactions was that of Sarah, my spider monkey. Her cage sat next to my bed, and she never stirred. She slept peacefully throughout the entire quake. Sarah's mind probably pulled up memories from her ancestors, leading her to dream that she was asleep high up in the forest canopy and a strong wind was blowing, causing the trees to sway!

A Dog, a Monkey and a Tortoise

Many years ago, Cypress Dog and Cat Hospital had outside dog runs so that hospitalized animals were able to go out and enjoy some fresh air and sunshine during their stay. Frank was a very old, black miniature poodle with a chronic ear infection. Frank's owners, Mr. & Mrs. Winston, a sweet retired couple in their late 60s, loved him dearly and brought him into the clinic every two to three weeks to have his ears cleaned. I don't think they were very diligent about using the medicine we always sent home with him, but at least they were willing to bring him in for regular care. They would drop Frank off in the morning, go play golf, and pick him up in the late afternoon. After we treated him, we would put him in one of the outside runs, but as he was pretty much deaf and blind, he couldn't fully appreciate our high-class facilities.

Sarah hanging out, enjoying breakfast (a slice of watermelon). She was a very cute baby.

One of Frank's ear-cleaning days coincided with the day before I was to leave town for several days, so I had brought Sarah, my monkey, in to board while I was gone. She was in one of the outside runs for the day and was fascinated by the dogs in the adjacent runs. She would reach her long arms or her tail through the chain link wire and play with the dogs. I wasn't worried she would hurt them as she had lived peacefully, and even playfully, with my dog Osa for several years. Except when Sarah was loose in the house, Osa always had the option to move outside the range of her cage. Sarah's neighbors in the hospital runs had the same option, by moving to the opposite side of their cages. I was curious to see how Frank would react to Sarah, since I was sure he had never seen a monkey before. Frank was not impressed. In fact, he did not react to Sarah at all, even when she was scratching his back. I guess since he couldn't "see" her, he was just happy to be petted.

Two months later, we had a desert tortoise come in for some x-rays and he spent the day with us. After his x-rays were taken, we thought that being a desert tortoise, he would prefer to be outside in the sun rather than in an inside cage. Frank was also there for his regular ear cleaning and we put the tortoise in the run next to Frank. Frank immediately started barking and wouldn't shut up. Finally, we brought him back inside the building. His bad eyes must have seen well enough to decide that a rock was moving and he wasn't happy with the situation. You just can't predict what animals will do.

Can I Come, Too?

When I bought Bam, I didn't yet have a corral on my property, so I kept him at a nearby stable. My friend Thelma Erickson and her three little red-headed pixies would sometimes go with me to visit and ride Bam. Even after once nearly falling off, Erin, the middle and most adventurous child, always led the cries of excitement when we headed over to see Bam. Young city girls being thrilled to go horseback riding certainly isn't news. All girls love horses, don't they? Well, these three girls were anything but your typical city kids. Orange County no longer had massive orange groves and ranch manors, but there remained a few large-for-the-city sized lots. Thelma, the girls and their dad, Willy, lived on one of these large lots, an acre of property smack dab in the middle of Garden Grove, which lay in the heart of the Orange County concrete jungle. Blindfolded and deposited in their backyard, you would have guessed you were anywhere but in a big city. If you ignored the sound of traffic, the jets flying overhead and the dark brown smog, you would have sworn you were on a farm out in the country.

The Ericksons grew their own vegetables and raised chickens, rabbits and pigs -- and everything ended up on the dining table in one form or another. If you grew up in Southern California, you might be a little, or a lot, taken aback by this, but if you were raised in Georgia, as Thelma and Willy were, it's just the way you did things. And it was very important to them to provide their children with a down-to-earth upbringing in the midst of the big-city sprawl.

For their part, Heather, 7, Erin, 6, and Kathy, 4, seemed to thrive in this environment. They helped with chores, like weeding the garden and collecting eggs, but they also embraced city life in their love for Disneyland, Knott's Berry Farm, the beach and the occasional visit to the video arcade. They really seemed to enjoy how impressed their friends were when they came to visit "Erickson Ranch," strutting around like roosters in a hen house, showing off all their animals and vegetables. The girls were very bright and quite worldly for their ages. They had learned about the "birds and the bees," having witnessed the chickens and the rabbits breeding, and while they loved the animals, they accepted that Wilbur the pig would one day be served for breakfast.

On one of our visits, I had given each of the girls a ride on Bam and they all helped me brush him before we put him back in his corral. Erin had just given him the last piece of a carrot and we had walked no more than ten feet toward our car when Bam decided he wanted to come with us and tried to come over the fence. Being trained as a jumper, he could have easily made it, but apparently had second thoughts mid-jump, remembering that uncommanded jumps were anything but rewarded. Or perhaps it was the lack of a proper running start. Whatever the reason for the incomplete effort, poor Bam ended up with his front feet on the ground outside the corral, his flank area (belly) hanging on the fence and his rear feet dangling above the ground back in the corral. In an earlier story, I noted what a smart horse Bam was, and after this brief lapse in judgment, he realized that he had made a stupid mistake and that he was in big trouble. He didn't panic and struggle to get free, seemingly understanding he would only hurt himself. He just stood/hung there waiting for someone to help him. The owner of the stable heard the commotion - coming mostly from the two women and three girls, not the horse - came over and assessed the situation. While the five of us soothed Bam, he went off to fetch some tools and came back and removed the fence rail from under Bam. Even I was impressed at how calm Bam remained, waiting until he was told to move and then calmly walking away from the mess. He waited more while the fence was rebuilt and then walked back into his repaired corral. Bam was a gelding, but I was still concerned about possible damage done by straddling the fence, but luckily, his only injury was his pride.

Poor Willy, an amazingly patient man – as one must be to live in a household with four rambunctious and headstrong women – was barraged with stories about the excitement of the afternoon, each one of us feeling compelled to share our special observation or insight into the event. The story had pretty much been brought to a close when Kathy, who was the youngest but no less bright or observant than her sisters, added, "And it's a good thing Bam's not Italian!" It took a few seconds before we burst out laughing, realizing Kathy didn't mean "Italian," she meant "stallion." Apparently, she too must have noticed the precarious position Bam's reproductive anatomy was in as he hung on the fence rail. In the end, my greatest amazement with this story is that a four-year-old knew the difference between a gelding and a stallion.

Short Surgery, Long Recovery

Figaro was a cat that I treated early in my career. Mr. and Mrs. Forester had adopted Figaro as a kitten in Thailand while Captain Forester was serving in the U.S. Army. Probably not too surprisingly, Figaro was Siamese. He lived with the Foresters in Thailand for three years before returning stateside with them. On one of the first days Figaro was allowed out of their Orange County house, he wandered out into the street and was hit by a car. Welcome to America.

Poor Figaro had a nasty fracture of his femur. I felt the fracture, took some x-rays and told the Foresters that I should be able to surgically repair the leg. My staff and I stayed until 10 p.m. and got his leg put back together with a pin and some wires. The surgery lasted almost three hours. Figaro was a trooper afterwards, putting up with the doubtless pain and the nuisance of a heavily splinted rear leg for several weeks. His leg healed marvelously, but the "land of the free" now included only the house and its screened-in porch. There would be no more learning the hazards of western civilization the hard way for Figaro.

Three months later, the Foresters brought him back to have the pin removed. This was a five-minute surgery. I gave him the anesthetic, pulled out the pin, and put a stitch in the little incision I had made. He never woke up. Why did he tolerate a three-hour surgery, but was not able to handle the five-minute procedure to remove the pin? I have never figured that out. It may have been the first, but certainly wasn't the last time I encountered inexplicably unfortunate reactions to anesthetic. Every incident (luckily, there haven't been many) has been a harsh reminder to never start any anesthetic procedure without concern for the outcome.

Good Dog ... Very Good Dog!

Butch was one such very good dog. The Jenkins family adopted Butch when he was a little puppy – "little" being a relative term, as Butch was a Great Dane and never was very little. From his early days, Butch, quite handsome with a fawn coat, mottled white chest and belly and black muzzle and ears, was always a people-loving, happy dog who got along with kids as well as adults. Butch was prone, however, to fits of exuberance underscored by extreme tail wagging. Perhaps his energy state would better be described by saying he had short fits of calm spotting his normal high-spirited state.

Whenever Butch stood up, he would literally empty table-tops with a couple of passes of his tail. Not only did the Jenkins quickly tire of picking things up, they were also afraid that such boisterousness could be dangerous for their eighteen-month-old son Brian should he come within wagging range. But they didn't want to banish poor Butch to the backyard just because he was overly lovable. So Butch was allowed to stay in the house, but only after they trained him to never to stand up while inside. Instead, he learned to do a military crawl. He would literally move from room to room by his crawling on his belly. I actually got to see this for myself, as it had been my suggestion, and the Jenkins were so impressed by the results of their training that they invited me over for dinner so I could see Butch in action. I've seen a lot of amazing animal tricks, but I burst out laughing as I watched Butch maneuver his way around the house, including up and down several stairs that led to their sunken family room. He reminded me of the movies I had seen of soldiers crawling, with the exception of his vigorously-wagging tail. Once outside or given the release word, Butch was allowed to stand and move about normally. But inside, staying down was the norm. This stance kept the household items intact and small children safe from inadvertent knockdowns. Butch had no problems with this arrangement which seemed ideal for everyone involved.

One morning, Mrs. Jenkins was on the phone visiting with a friend. She heard Butch whining in the other room and called to him to be quiet. Her conversation continued and so did Butch's whining. "Butch, be quiet!" she shouted again. After several more minutes, Butch was still whining so Mrs. Jenkins got off the phone and went to deal with the dog. As she walked into the room she found Brian straddling Butch's neck sticking a pencil down into his ear. Blood was pouring out of the ear, but Butch would not stand up and break the house rules. He would not get up to get away from the little terror intent on trying to stick a pencil all the way through his head. He simply laid there and whined.

Luckily a dog's ear structure is such that the pencil never got to the ear drum. Butch's hearing was unaffected by this small mishap, except perhaps to make it more acute so he was able to disappear quickly – as quickly as a 130-pound Great Dane can – at the slightest sound of an approaching small child, aka Brian.

Let Sleeping Dogs Lie

Over the years, I've had the good fortune to have several incredibly special dogs as pets. Although it's hard, and perhaps not fair, to compare them, I must admit that Osa, a one-hundred-pound Newfoundland, is probably my all-time favorite. For such a large dog, Osa was exceptionally gentle. For several years, she had her own pet rabbit, Ruff, who would curl up right under her chin. Picturing downy-soft, beige-brown Ruff with his floppy ears looking so small, vulnerable and yet totally at peace snuggled up with Osa with her long, black-matte coat and her own floppy ears makes me smile. Osa was also amazingly patient with kids – even those that climbed all over her and insisted on tugging at her ears and tail. Cliché though it is, she wouldn't hurt a flea.

When she was about five years old, Osa developed a small tumor under her tongue, so I took her to work with me to remove it. She calmly allowed Briana and Jenny, my technicians and two of her favorite people, to wrestle her up onto the operating table and hardly flinched when I inserted the needle to anesthetize her. Excising the tumor involved a relatively simple surgery where I slit the surface of the tongue, cut around the tumor to free it, and stitched closed the surface. The surgery went well and as I was finishing, Osa was starting to wake up – standard procedure and good anesthetic technique. I reached back into her mouth one last time to check the stitches when she was suddenly awake enough to clamp her mouth tightly shut. Unfortunately, my hand was in the way – not standard procedure or good post-operative technique! She made a nice hole in my palm, one that immediately turned bright red, but amazingly only issued a trickle of blood. Nonetheless, I passed out and slumped to the floor, leaving Briana and Jenny in a quandary. Do they take care of the large dog waking up on the table or do they take care of the veterinarian passed out on the floor? They made the right decision – they ignored me and got Osa off the table and into a cage before she finished waking up. Osa's tumor was benign and she recovered quickly. My hand did not recover as quickly – it was sore for several weeks. The puncture was clean, however, so there was no infection. If I look carefully, I can still see the scar – a reminder to be careful when and where I put my hand.

Edgar Allen Poe, the Crow

Shortly before we got married, Tom showed up at my place for dinner carrying a medium-sized moving box. I hadn't asked him to bring anything for dinner, wine didn't come in that size box, and it wasn't any day that usually earned a present. I'm game to receive a gift any day, but it wasn't wrapped – not that I'm too particular about that, either. What might it be? Tom kept a straight face as I looked questioningly from the box to his face and back to the box again. Then the box started screaming! Like a real showman, Tom dramatically opened the top off the box, exclaiming, "Ta Da!" I peered in to see an adult crow. Definitely not what I expected!

Tom had been out for his daily run and had seen several young boys chasing a crow. It couldn't fly, so Tom confiscated the bird and brought it to me. The crow had a broken wing that had healed improperly, such that he would never be able to fly. He was quite tame. I guessed he had been adopted by someone while his wing healed and that person had just released him without verifying that he could fly. So Edgar Allen Poe the Crow – Tom was very clever with animal names – became a member of our family.

Poe lived in the back yard with Osa the dog, Gabby the goat, and Bam the horse. It seemed like quite a crew of pets, but these were the early days that I would occasionally look back on, dreaming of how simple feeding time was. Since Poe couldn't fly, we were confident he would stay in the yard. He liked to steal food from Osa's dish, but she was very easy going and was quite willing to share with him, especially since he didn't take much. His favorite hangout was on top of the hay bales we kept under an eave on the back porch. I had hay delivered by the truckload, and would store it on the back porch to keep it dry, taking a single bale at a time to a small enclosure (mini-barn) by Bam's corral.

We soon discovered why Poe had such an affinity for the hay – he used it to store his treasures, the many items he pilfered from around the backyard. When he found a bent nail, a pencil eraser, bottle cap or similar object in the yard, he would scurry over to the hay, hop up to the one that was currently serving as his treasure chest, poke a little hole in the hay with his beak, and then insert his new-found prize. He would always fill the hole with more hay so no one could see his hiding place. Once a week, Tom would drag a new bale of hay over to the barn for me to feed to Bam. Occasionally he would take the bale that had Poe's treasures in, causing Poe to panic. He would follow Tom all the way to the barn, squawking the whole way. Once his treasure chest was in its new home in the barn, Poe would extract his cache of valuables one by one, carry them back to the bales of hay under the eaves and put them in a fresh bale. It may seem mean to cause him such distress every few weeks, but he did an exceptional job of hiding his hoard. Unless we made note when we saw him hiding something, we didn't know which bale was "his."

Watching him with his treasures in the hay was fun. Unfortunately he also liked to hide treasures in the lounge pads on the patio. Worse yet, he had to make a new hole for each item, pull out some stuffing, put in his booty, and replace the stuffing. I didn't enjoy having holes in my lounge pads, and I didn't enjoy being chased away from the lounge if I chose to sit in one that he was using for treasure storage!

Poe protecting the treasures he hid in the lounge pad.

Sometimes You Gotta Break the Rules

Osa was buddies with my parents' teacup poodle, Peanut, allowing him to hang from her ears. The term "buddies" definitely didn't apply to her relationship with Coquette, my dad's black miniature poodle. There were other dogs in the household, but Coquette belonged to Dad, and he to her. She was very protective and constantly strove to keep other dogs, including Osa, away from him. At first, she insinuated herself between Osa and Dad. When that didn't produce the desired effect, she turned to snarling and snapping. Osa, the loving giant she was, seemed very confused by these rebukes, but relented. Over the years, Coquette became more and more protective, to the point that she didn't even want Osa in the same room. Osa, too, changed with age, growing out of her naiveté. She would back off when Coquette snarled, but the look on her face turned from one of hurt to one of open distaste and disdain.

When Osa was five or six, Dad had a major heart attack. He was forty-eight and had been homesick for his boyhood home for some time, so Mom, Mikey and he moved to the bluegrass region of Kentucky. I was born in Lexington and loved horses, so I was excited to go visit them and the Thoroughbreds that the region is famous for. I took Osa everywhere with me, so naturally, she came along. If I had warned her we were going to see her cousins, she might have elected to stay home. The move to Kentucky hadn't done anything to improve Coquette's disposition. She spent the first two days of our visit sitting by my Dad, growling at Osa. I'm a vet, and she was a female dog, so I'm allowed to say it - what a bitch!

On Sunday morning, the third day of my visit, Mom fixed a delicious big breakfast. As was their normal practice, the dogs all laid at our feet, mentally willing food to jump off our plates and into their mouths. It worked some of the time. After we had devoured all the food, we stayed at the table, relaxing and chatting. Sensing the food was gone, Coquette returned to her vigil of guarding Dad. I don't know if something in particular triggered it, or if Osa had finally had enough of the snarling fuzzball, but as we all sat and watched, she leaned forward, grabbed Coquette around the chest and picked her up. I have spent most of my veterinary career telling clients not to reach into a dog fight with their hands, to use only inanimate objects. But this was my dad's favorite dog that my dog was holding in her mouth. I was financially independent and married, but I instinctively knew that our relationship would not survive if Osa bit down too hard. I broke my rules, straddled Osa, grabbed her mouth, pried it open and shook Coquette out of it.

Coquette had four bite wounds, two on each side of her chest, but none were deep enough to require more than routine treatment. Dad put aside any anger he might have felt at the moment, fetched his doctor's bag and assisted me in treating the punctures. For the remaining two days of that visit I was tense, fearing another encounter that might not turn out as well. I kept Osa right by my side at all times. Whenever Coquette came into the same room with us, which was noticeably less often than normal, she stayed as far away from Osa as possible. She may have been nasty, but she wasn't totally stupid. No way was she going to harass that big dog again!

Here, Hold This

After vet school I did quite well for several years and actually practiced veterinary medicine for almost five years without fainting. In late spring 1974, I was working with another vet, Dr. Jack Cruz, examining Jacques, a six-year-old gray miniature poodle with an infected inner ear. Normally, one of us would have performed this procedure with the aid of a technician, but it was a slow day and we enjoyed the opportunity to work together, even on relatively simple cases. Perhaps it was because we were both young vets and appreciated the reassurance of collaboration.

Apparently Jacques' ear infection had spread far enough to cause extreme sensitivity out on the ear flap, because as I lifted it up so I could look in his ear, he yelped and bit me, somehow managing to clamp down deep into the webbing between the thumb and forefinger of my left hand. I immediately had a great and very personal appreciation for his painful ear, as that part of the hand is also quite sensitive. At the moment however, my thoughts did not move toward sympathy for the ailing poodle. Fortunately for Jacques, nor did they advance to rage and retribution. Actually, those thoughts might have passed briefly through my brain, but they were quickly short-circuited as I – surprise – passed out.

This would not be particularly noteworthy considering my history, were it not for the fact that I was eight and half months pregnant with Allie. Poor Dr. Cruz was in a total panic – not that I noticed – trying to figure out how to keep me from falling while not knowing where or how to hold such a very pregnant woman! He never explained how he got me to the floor, but I did sense that he was more embarrassed by the incident than I was, and I was the one that fainted. However it was that he managed, Dr. Cruz, Allie, and I – and Jacques – all survived unharmed. Jacques' infection was resolved with the aid of a strong pain killer and a muzzle followed by a two week course of ear ointment and antibiotics. I worked a little while longer before Allie was born, but Dr. Cruz didn't work with me again. I wonder why?

Quillie Acres Veterinary Clinic

People-Puppy

When Tom and I got married, I told him that I would not give up the practice of veterinary medicine to be a wife and mother. At the same time, I wanted to raise my own children and not depend on babysitters. And I sometimes wondered why my kids were so headstrong! We decided that I could do both (i.e., Tom gave in gracefully). So, two weeks before Allie was born, I quit my job at Cypress Dog and Cat Hospital with the plan to start my own part-time practice in a few months. I was very sad to leave, but I was also anxious to have the baby, especially since summer had arrived early, its heat making the last month of my pregnancy quite miserable.

A few weeks after Allie arrived, I returned to Cypress Dog and Cat to fill in for a week while Dr. Cruz took a short vacation. I was nursing Allie, so I brought her with me, figuring she would sleep a lot since she was just a few weeks old. She was my first, so I hadn't learned yet how naïve that idea was, as any mothers reading this might have guessed. The first few days went smoothly, as Allie did indeed sleep a lot and was very well behaved most of the time. Late Thursday morning, though, she was fussy and generally expressing her displeasure at being left alone in the second exam room while I was seeing a patient in the

67

first. The owner of the cat I was examining had been a client for several years and knew that I had left to have a baby. He heard the noises from next door and with a half smirk, half smile asked "Is that a people-puppy I hear?" I cracked up, not having heard that term before.

My people-puppy usually slept in her baby carrier in the second exam room, but later that day Killer, a not-very-nice Australian Shepherd, had to pass through Allie's room to get to the x-ray machine. My recently-developed maternal instincts kicked in, causing me to worry that Killer might knock Allie over or worse yet, try to bite her. Pam, the veterinary technician, had the answer. Rather than try to play musical rooms with Allie, she simply picked up the carrier and put it in a large dog cage – with Allie in it! She was completely safe and didn't complain. Well, that is, until years later to her therapist.

()()

Taking the Show on the Road

When I finished covering for Dr. Cruz's vacation, I spent another couple of months being "just a mom" before I started my own practice. The decision to strike out on my own had not been precipitated by my pregnancy alone. For several years, I had served as the relief veterinarian for the only vet in the area that treated goats and sheep. As a result of his untimely death a year earlier, I became the only one in the region with any experience or willingness to treat small ruminants. I had been handling this work on my days off, but when I became pregnant, I saw it as an ideal opportunity to open my own practice, work only part-time and continue to support my existing small livestock clients. They would serve as a foundation on which to build my own small animal practice. Thus, what would eventually be known as Quillie Acres Veterinary Clinic was born. (The name itself came later, as Quillie is a made-up word, formed from Quin and Allie, the names of my two children.) The creative naming may not have come for a few years, but the creative thinking didn't wait.

In addition to the traditional sheep and goats, I also treated llamas, wallabies, and alpacas. On occasion, I traveled to the client's home to treat a large collection of animals. Even the owners of a single goat or sheep lamented that it was often difficult to transport their animals, especially when they were sick, and thought it would be a superb idea for me to come to them instead. When several of my dog-owning clients agreed it would be nice to have the veterinarian come to the house and save the mental trauma (for both pets and owners) of trips to the clinic, I decided to make my practice mobile.

I bought a new, 1975 orange (my favorite color) and white Dodge Tradesman high-roof van, and Tom converted it to function marvelously as a mobile veterinary clinic. He equipped it with supply cabinets, a locking drug cabinet, a refrigerator, and even a hydraulic operating table (which Tom's brother Bob had bought as a throw-in item at a machinist's auction). There was another key piece of customization – accommodation for baby Allie. The one-time use of an animal cage while subbing at Cypress Dog and Cat Hospital served a purpose, but was out of the question here. However, I wanted to leave the passenger seat available for an assistant. So, Tom built a special platform for Allie's car seat just behind the passenger seat. This way, she was within arm's reach of me or the passenger, but she was safely out of harm's way.

So the as yet unnamed Quillie Acres Veterinary Clinic was not only in business, but it had wheels. For about a dozen years, my "clinic on wheels" traveled to clients' ranches, farms and homes all over Southern California.

Don't Worry, It's Only my Little Brother

My mom and dad had four children, but they spread us way out. I am the eldest (I always told them that they should have stopped with just one child). Mikey, the youngest, is fourteen years younger than I am. That age difference allowed us to become good friends without too much sibling rivalry, although it took him some time to learn that his big sister was much easier to get along with if she won at ping pong.

When he was fifteen, Mikey was living with me for the summer, taking driver's education at the local high school and working as my veterinary assistant. One of the advantages of having your assistant living in your house, especially when he is your little brother, is that you can conveniently call him into work at any hour. Just such an occasion arose late one evening when Mrs. Morgan called, worried that Bentley, her rather cantankerous male cat, was being more ill-tempered than normal. She had observed that the very large orange and white tabby was straining to urinate, but his litter box was staying dry. I immediately diagnosed a plugged bladder, which is not only uncomfortable for the cat, but dangerous if left untreated for too long, so I told Mrs. Morgan to load up Bentley and bring him right over.

Mikey and I met Mrs. Morgan and Bentley as they drove up the driveway, and we all climbed into my hospital van. The typical "June gloom" (fog) had settled in, making for a damp and chilly night. I live in Southern California because I don't like the cold, so we closed the van door to keep in the heat and to keep Bentley from escaping. In spite of my intention to ease their pain and discomfort, I've learned that my patients are generally not convinced of this and tend to squirm, slither or race away when I start pressing on sore spots and sticking them with needles. I offered to let Mrs. Morgan wait in the house, but she wanted to watch and said she was even willing to help. Knowing that this would be a clean process (i.e., no blood and therefore no worry about her becoming queasy) and realizing that one more person in the van to provide body heat would warm it up that much faster, I accepted her offer.

I checked Bentley over and found that indeed his bladder was very full and hard. It was fully distended with urine because he had stones blocking his urethra and therefore could not urinate. I anesthetized him, and Mikey kept a watch on his vital signs while I worked to remove the offending stones. When all goes well with this procedure and you get the last stone removed, the urine just starts to flow. It usually flows fast and furious because the bladder has been so distended and has built up a lot of pressure. Bentley was an intact tom cat and his urine was very strong smelling as it gushed out and into the collection tray. I looked up from the cat to brag about what a good job I had done for Bentley when I noticed that Mikey was a bit pale. His eyes weren't focused and he was starting to sway. He was on the other side of the operating table from me, so I reached across and grabbed the front of his shirt, helping to slow his collapse to the floor. Once he was as far down as I could lower him, I let go and turned my attention back to Bentley, who was still asleep on the table. Mrs. Morgan was quite concerned and asked if I shouldn't be doing something more for Mikey. I told her that he had just fainted and would be fine. Her cat was a much higher priority at that time. Mikey woke up shortly thereafter and was very embarrassed. I, with the help of Tom, have made sure he never lives down his lack of tolerance for certain smells. Since he wasn't hurt, I can admit that I was selfishly pleased to learn that I wasn't the only one in the family that was prone to fainting.

I Say "Uncle"!

My little brother Mikey was my first veterinary assistant. He attended school in the morning and in the afternoon, he, Allie and I took off in the van to see my clients and their pets. There was a special bond between Allie and her Uncle Mike – a bond that remains today – so having a combination assistant and babysitter worked marvelously. After having worked solo for a year, I enjoyed having the extra hands. I've had at least one assistant ever since.

During this summer, in an attempt to combat the heart problems that run in my family and the general malaise that besets teenagers, my marathon-running husband

Tom encouraged (i.e., prodded, pushed and nagged) Mikey to join him for his after-work runs. For the first few weeks, Tom would drag Mikey along for his warm-up, and then send him home gasping and wheezing while he went on to do a real workout. By the end of the summer, Mikey worked up to running the full course, but by the time he arrived home, Tom had showered and was enjoying a cocktail.

When Mikey returned to Santa Cruz after the summer, a friend recruited him to run on the high school cross country team. Tom was quite pleased that his efforts might have a lasting effect. Little did he realize how much effect he had. That November, when Mikey and my parents came to our house for Thanksgiving, he challenged Tom to a race. So, Tom confidently mapped out his favorite five-mile course. But he quietly confided to me before the race started, "Mikey will probably be back sipping on a soda before I finish." Much to our surprise, Mikey not only showed up first, but Tom was not in sight. Although he was so exhausted he could barely stand, we herded him into the house, into his clothes and shoved a soda in his hand just as Tom came into the finish. The effect was not lost on Tom, who grumbled some sort of acknowledgment on his way to the shower.

The stakes of what would become the annual "Turkey Trot" increased when Uncle Mike presented Tom with a turkey trophy with his name engraved on it. Try as he might over the next several years, Tom was never able to "lose" the trophy.

What does all this have to do with my veterinary practice or my many and varied pets (i.e., the subject of this book)? Well, during the years of the annual Turkey

Trot, one of our pets came to us courtesy of a community raffle. We were one of the "winners." Our prize ... a turkey ... a live male turkey! A "tom." What shall we name this new member of our family? Naming it Tom seemed too obvious and might have been confusing since we already had one "Tom" in the family. Uncle Mike didn't live with us any longer, and although he never won the turkey trophy, we all considered him an honorary turkey. Our new pet was thus named "Uncle Mike."

"Uncle Mike," the turkey - the one that isn't my brother.

Weasel out of This

Ferrets, who are members of the weasel family, are illegal to own in California, but a 1996 survey by the American Veterinary Medical Association put their population at over one hundred thousand. Yes, over one hundred thousand! Before you call the I.N.S. to get rid of these illegal aliens, know that they are legal as pets in forty-eight states, the exceptions being California and Hawaii. In the late 1800s, Hawaii actually imported a cousin of the ferret, the mongoose, in a failed attempt to combat the rat population. Mongooses were assumed to be nocturnal, as are rats, but they are actually diurnal (active during the day) and thus they found other food sources. To make matters worse, the mongoose has no natural predator on the islands, so the population has thrived. Thus, it is somewhat understandable that Hawaii is reluctant to allow a similar animal into their closed system. There is no such lack of predators in California, though, which is part of the reason why you don't see these relatives of the weasel inundating our neighborhoods or the wild.

My introduction to ferrets came from Tammy Higgins. She called late one night because Timmy was sick. She told me on the phone that she had this "animal" that she needed me to see. After significant prodding and blanket assurances on my part, she eventually told me Timmy was a ferret. She had purchased him in Nevada and driven across the state line with him hidden in a bag (like they check!). This occurred in 1975 and Timmy was the first ferret I had ever seen. Tammy brought him in because he had been crawling under some furniture and had a small laceration over his shoulder. He was a very personable young ferret. I anesthetized him, sewed up his wound and sent him home with Tammy. Of course, I had to promise that I would not tell anyone about him.

When she came back in two weeks to have his sutures removed, she kept him in his little carrying bag until she was in my exam room with the door closed – so no one else would see him. As time went on, Tammy became much more relaxed about her ferret, eventually letting him nose around the waiting room in his harness and leash. I also began to see many more of them as patients. I always found that first-time clients would call to make an appointment, but would not tell my receptionist that it was for a ferret. They would call their pet a "funny cat," or "my pet," but would not say the word "ferret" over the phone. They were in no danger of me turning them into Fish and Game, as I was so taken by Timmy that I ended up with two of my own – Madison and Farrah. They were very fun pets, as they were cuddly but also very playful. It was a blast to watch them scamper around the floor, always looking for small openings to squeeze into and investigate, and it was a real crack-up to watch one mock-fight some imaginary foe. I figure it's safe to publish this now, as Madison, Farrah and Timmy have all been gone long enough to have exceeded the statute of limitations for owning them in California.

Back in the seventies, Tammy was sufficiently concerned (i.e., paranoid) that she called the State Fish and Game Department to find out exactly what would happen if she were caught with her illegal pets – she had gotten another one to keep Timmy company. She went to a pay phone to make the call. She talked to Mr. Ranger and explained that she had two ferrets; she knew they were illegal, but what would happen to them if they were caught and confiscated. Mr. Ranger discussed all the aspects of the ferret laws with Tammy. He was very polite and even explained that if she were never reported that they would never know about her. He knew there were many ferrets in Orange County. When she asked where she could find a copy of the rules and regulations about ferrets, he asked for her name and address and offered to mail her a copy. She laughed and told him there was no way she was giving him her name and address. He finally gave her the appropriate names and article numbers so she could look up the information. I don't think Mr. Ranger ever realized that Tammy had called him from a pay phone rather than her home phone, as that was well before the advent of Caller ID!

Madison demonstrating a ferret's affinity for squeezing into tight spaces.

My Weight is None of Your Business

John and Susie Glenn, a real estate developer and a pediatrician, both in their mid-forties, had a five-acre ranch in a remote part of Orange County, where they lived with their children Amy, seven, and Madison, four, two horses, Countess and Charisma, two Doberman Pinschers, Dirk and Diana, and two llamas, Cleopatra and Hannibal. They seemed to like things in pairs. A few more pairs of animals and they could build their own ark. Hannibal was a beautiful and well behaved animal, but they knew that he would be a much nicer pet if he was neutered. There had never been a problem, but for the safety of the girls, they decided to err on the side of caution and have Hannibal castrated. John loaded him into a horse trailer and dropped him off at my clinic early in the morning on his way to work. Surgery was scheduled for 10 am, so we put Hannibal in a stall to wait his turn.

By this time, I had converted my barn into a fully functional clinic and was only rarely using the van to travel to clients' homes. Two kids were too many to haul around with me. The waiting room of my clinic was the center aisle of the barn, a ten-foot-wide by twenty-foot-long area of decomposed granite largely covered by brown indoor-outdoor carpet, with a park bench and a couple of chairs on one side and a large platform scale, used to weigh my patients, on the other.

The office, examining room, surgery room, recovery room, storage room, and x-ray lab were at the back end of this aisle. Lest you start imagining an expansive, multi-room facility, all these rooms totaled about 300 square feet. The office was more of a cubbyhole, with a desk pushed up against a Dutch-door, which opened to the waiting area. The examination room was six feet wide and nine feet deep with the exam table protruding out from one wall, also opened directly onto the waiting area. If you walked behind the cubbyhole office, you came to the eight-foot-wide by nine-foot-deep surgery room. Off the other side of the examination room were the recovery, storage and x-ray rooms, which were really one multi-purpose room. Nothing large was stored there. It wasn't physically possible.

My house and garage served as the storage areas for bulk items. In the clinic's storage room, we kept mostly medications and some of the surgical and examination supplies that wouldn't fit in their respective rooms. The recovery room consisted of two cages below one of the storage cabinets, and next to them was the x-ray machine, well shielded to protect any pets that happened to be in recovery when we x-rayed another. The closet across from the x-ray machine served as the x-ray processing lab.

Contrasting the cramped quarters inside the clinic, on either side of the waiting room were two twelve-by-twelve stalls, originally designed for horses. We added wire mesh to the lower portion of two of the stalls, making them suitable for small dogs. A third stall was split into three narrow stalls, allowing me to restrain a larger patient and even approach it from the adjacent pen. The fourth stall remained a horse stall, with a gate out to the main corral, allowing my retired show-horse, Bam, pony, Raffles, and mule, Annie, to keep an eye on my clients and patients. This stall was directly adjacent to the examining room door, so occasionally Bam would stick his head through the door to observe the goings-on.

Hannibal got one of the large stalls to himself. When the time came for his surgery, we led him to the scale outside his stall. I needed to weigh him so I could give him just the right amount of anesthetic. Llamas are very fluffy, and I didn't want to guess his weight wrong. After several minutes arguing with him, we finally got him positioned on the scale, but the scale didn't work. It had been fine earlier in the morning when we weighed a Great Dane, but it wasn't working now. A minor amount of checking found the problem. Hannibal's stall had been the one right next to the scale. While he was waiting in the morning, he had amused himself by chewing through the wires to the display head of the scale! Having the display at eye level was extremely convenient. Trying to look over and around a large pig or sticking your head between the legs of a goat or llama to read a normal scale is not very practical, nor a good idea. As great a design as it was, we had overlooked the destructive nature of some of our patients, and the scale was non-functional. Hannibal didn't win, though, and I didn't have to compromise my principle that accurate weight is very important when administering anesthesia. Hannibal had been in for a minor, unrelated, non-surgical procedure about six months earlier, and we had weighed him then. I was confident his weight had not changed appreciably and dosed him appropriately. He still had his surgery, and it went fine.

On his way home from work that evening, John returned to pick up Hannibal. He laughed with us but was a bit red-faced when we described what Hannibal had done. To his credit, he offered to pay for the repair, but I declined, admitting that it was my responsibility to protect against such incidents.

The next day, Jeff, my office manager Donna's husband, came and rewired the scale. I was glad Jeff could do the repair because I knew he did excellent work and understood animals. Plus, I could pay him by providing free service on his and Donna's collection of pets. Just the same, it would have been fun to see the reaction of an electrician as I explained how my scale got damaged. Jeff was very thorough, wisely covering the wires in a hard plastic sheath to help protect them in the future. I knew that another llama could chew through the hard plastic too, but hoped that we would notice what he was doing before he caused damage to the wires. We actually were even smarter than that. We put future llamas in a stall that wasn't within reach of the scale wires.

Advantages of a Small Town

Although Orange Park Acres (OPA) is but an overgrown subdivision in vast Orange County, living in OPA was like living in a small town. It had the same advantages – you knew everyone and what they were doing. It also had the same disadvantages – everyone knew you and what you were doing. Even with the occasional unfounded rumor, I really did like the small town atmosphere. One reason why was that since all your neighbors knew what you were doing, they also knew when you needed help, and a surprising number of our neighbors were actually willing to provide that help.

On a warm, sunny August afternoon, soon after we had moved into Orange Park Acres, I went for a horseback ride with our new neighbors, Esther and Sam. It was the weekend, so Tom stayed home with Allie, then just over two, and Quin, my son, who was only five months old. As we were cantering along a trail, Bam, my fifteen-year-old quarter horse gelding, tripped and we both fell. Bam had been marvelously well trained by Doris, my old college roommate and an Olympic-caliber horsewoman. She had used Bam as a training horse but retired him to my care as an eight-year-old when Tom and I bought our first horse-friendly (i.e., corral, small barn and nearby horse trails) house in Villa Park. So, Bam and I had forged a very strong bond by the time he was fifteen, and I would enjoy another fifteen years of his company.

Even considering Bam's terrific training, I was amazed and immensely gratified that he somehow twisted himself and ended up falling so that he did not land on me. I'll admit that I probably was not immediately so appreciative of his athletic maneuver, as I landed on my left shoulder and broke my collarbone. I was hurting miserably and feeling quite sorry for myself, but I was also quite concerned for Bam who came up lame on his right front leg. Fortunately we were on a part of the trail that was not too far from civilization. In this particular area, the trail was in a culvert that acted as a wash during heavy rains, and it ran parallel to and below one of the neighborhood roads. This being well before the days of cell phones, Esther stayed with the horses and me while Sam headed off on the half-mile trek to where he knew there was a pay phone. He called his mother-in-law who was at his house, and she went next door to my house and baby-sat my kids (along with Esther and Sam's two older children) so Tom could take me to the hospital

.

While Esther and I were waiting down in the culvert, Donna and Bob Reynolds, two other OPA residents, were driving home on a street that overlooked our position. Bob was a local fireman and Donna was a horse trainer. Donna happened to notice that there were two people and three horses down in the culvert and decided that there must be a problem. I had never met Donna or Bob, and Esther only knew them casually, but they pulled over to the side of the road and clambered down the little side-hill to where Esther and I were waiting. Sam returned from the pay phone about five minutes later and explained that Tom was on his way. Sam had found a gate that he could open so Tom could drive into the culvert and save me from trying to climb up the side-hill, so he went back up to the road to flag down Tom.

Esther had already looked at my posture and decided that I must have broken my collar bone. Bob, who had been at the scene of many accidents, agreed with her diagnosis. With my status determined, we turned our attention to Bam. We all looked at his lame leg, but didn't detect any major injury, so Donna offered to ride him home while I went to the hospital. If he was too lame, she promised to get off and walk him. Esther and Sam rode behind her to observe.

Bam just had a sprain and was almost normal by the time he got home – a nice reward for trying so valiantly to protect me. I, on the other hand, was x-rayed, verified to have a fractured collar bone and sent home in a figure-eight splint to hold my shoulders back so the bone would heal properly. So, that seems like a very pleasant story about a small town and helpful neighbors. But wait! There's more.

The figure-eight splint left me unable to lift Quin…and I was nursing him! Being long past the age of wet nurses, there was no way my neighbors could directly alleviate this problem. Tom used pillows to prop the baby up so he could nurse and then, when I beckoned, came and switched him to the other side, and eventually burped him and put him back in his crib. Luckily, Quin was not nursing frequently at that age, but it was still a very awkward situation, and it required Tom to take a couple of weeks of belated paternity leave from work.

The local 4-H goat group heard about my injury through the grapevine. They decided to help by bringing us a fully-cooked dinner each night for the first week. Tom was thrilled – he wasn't much of a cook. This goodwill gesture took quite a load off him. Allie was thrilled – because Tom wasn't much of a cook – and she loved all the attention she got from whoever delivered the meals. At the end of that week, one of the families helped out even more than expected. Kathy Ramsey and Lola, her eleven-year-old daughter, brought dinner and stayed to serve it for us. They asked if there was anything else they could do since they knew I had been laid up for a week. They were delighted when I asked if they would be willing to bathe the baby. Tom changed diapers fine and made sure that Quin was fed, but he was either not willing or afraid to bathe him.

To better understand Tom with children, I have to take you back two years to when Allie, our eldest, was a newborn just home from the hospital. My parents were down to meet their first grandchild, and my mom planned to stay and help out for a week or two. The first afternoon we were home, Tom was on the couch holding Allie, with my mom sitting next to him, while I was off in the kitchen. Allie started crying, leaving

Tom, already very uncomfortable holding a baby, quite flustered. With more than a touch of desperation in his voice, he asked my mom, "What should I do?" Having plenty of experience with her own four kids, she instructed him to "put her in a more comfortable position." With little hesitation, Tom reached over and set Allie in my mom's arms! He has always been a loving and caring father, but was never terribly comfortable handling the kids when they were babies.

Kathy, Lola and Quin all thoroughly enjoyed the bath, and I was certainly glad to have small town neighbors willing to help out.

Here, Hold This II

Gina Jeffries was a local high school student – a junior, I believe – and a senior member of the local 4-H Club that my two young children would join a few years later. Allie, then five years old, absolutely idolized Gina. Gina's first 4-H project, when she was in junior high, was a veal calf, but for the preceding three years, she had been raising Suffolk sheep, a black-faced, black-legged breed. By this time, her herd consisted of five ewes and one ram. Gina managed the breeding, attended to the deliveries, docked tails and castrated her baby rams – impressive for an adult; even more so for a seventeen-year-old. She was a very knowledgeable young woman and a very competent shepherd.

Gina's one ram, Bruiser, was exceptionally-high quality according to the breed standard. Thus, Gina used him not only to breed her own ewes, but she also accepted outside ewes for him. The stud fees helped support her sheep business, but it also added the responsibility of caring for someone else's ewes. Bruiser was good at his job. He was very protective of his ewes and would not allow any humans into the pen with them – except for Gina. Bruiser loved Gina. She would climb into the pen, call, "Here Kitty, Kitty, Kitty" and Bruiser would abandon his current favorite ewe and come stand docilely in front of Gina, waiting to be scratched and loved. Once she haltered him, even I, a villainous veterinarian (or so it seemed many animals thought), could enter the pen and do whatever examination was required. I was amazed at how good Gina was with her sheep.

She was also an outstanding student, doing well in school and continuously growing her knowledge of livestock. She eventually became a successful pediatrician. This particular year, she had read that rather than castrating her ram lambs when they were only days old, she should wait until they were several months old. This would allow them to develop more fully and look better in the show ring.

She chose to test this theory on one of her best lambs and brought him to me for castration surgery when he was four months old. Since she was an old hand at this, I asked if she would help me with the surgery. "Of course!" she enthusiastically replied. I anesthetized the lamb, clipped and cleaned the scrotum and made my incision. Gina held his leg up out of the way while I did this. After I had exposed one testicle, I asked her to hold it, too, while I tied off the blood vessels. She gave me a blank look that said I had asked too much. She took hold of the testicle for a second, but she could not hold on. Not only did she have to drop the testicle, but also let go of the leg and went to the cab of her truck to lie down. At least she didn't do anything really embarrassing, like pass out. Luckily, my brother Mikey was visiting at the time and happened to come up to the clinic at that very moment. He held the leg and the testicles for me while I finished the surgery. I don't think that holding a lamb's leg and testicles was what he had in mind when he stopped by, as I think he was really there to see Gina. But it worked out for him, as he thoroughly enjoyed teasing Gina about her inability to assist.

I Thought You were my Friend

I believe "Uncle Mike," the turkey, was the only pet I won, aside from carnival goldfish. The more common way for my menagerie to grow in an unplanned manner was for one of my neighbors to bring an injured animal to my door – one of the downsides to running my practice out of my barn. I was like the local animal shelter, except I never developed an effective placement program, so our family grew with each Good Samaritan act. You would think that my friend and next door neighbor would have picked up on my dismay with each addition (although I quickly grew to love and enjoy each one) and also want to limit the number of animals living next door, but even she was guilty of dumping wounded critters on me.

The Frankfurters and their teenage daughter and son lived next door on an acre and a half lot, similar to ours.

Trudy and her daughter Rose were avid horsewomen, so whereas our yard was poorly maintained grass bordered by orange trees and goat pens, their yard was dominated by a riding arena and eight horse stalls. Rose loved her horses, and when she wasn't at school or doing homework, she could usually be found riding. In spite of Rose's passion for horses, much of the routine care of them fell to Trudy. One spring morning, while down tending to the horses, Trudy found a baby ground squirrel on the ground (I guess that makes sense) in front of the stalls. Naturally, her love of all animals and maternal instinct kicked in at the discovery of this homeless baby and led to a knock on my door. The little squirrel was just a couple of weeks old and still should have been nursing. I took her inside and borrowed a miniature baby bottle from one of Allie's dolls to feed her. Between being a vet and having a variety of pets, I always have a supply of formula on hand.

When Allie and Quin got home from kindergarten and pre-school, without hesitation, they named her Princess Leia. Guess which movie had just come out? ("Star Wars," of course) Leia took to bottle feeding very quickly. In between bottles, she liked to sleep under the collar of my shirt with her nose peeking out the front and the tip of her tail just hanging out at the back. Yes, they are quite small when they're young. I was faintly alarmed the first time she started to snuggle under my collar, but quickly found it completely adorable. Plus, it turned out to be extremely convenient, as I always knew where she was. (When Leia was older, I sometimes wished she, and her then much longer bushy tail, still liked to cuddle around my neck, especially on chilly mornings. What a nice muffler she would have made!)

As with most young things – my own kids included – she outgrew her completely adorable and dependent stage and became more adventurous and inquisitive. When I sat at my desk, Leia loved to crawl around and check out the pens, loose papers, paperclips, etc. Sometimes she reminded me of a kitten, except rather than bat at everything with a paw, she used her nose to nudge her new-found toys, and eventually her sharp little teeth to taste everything. At that point, playing on the desk was no longer allowed.

At family dinner time, she would venture off my shoulder and onto the table, moving from plate to plate deciding what was best to eat. She was tiny, didn't eat much, and was so cute that we all gladly shared. She had good taste, because her favorite was corn on the cob, from corn I grew in our backyard. It was sweet and delicious. The first time she tried to eat off the cob reminded me of a log-rolling contest, with a spinning corn cob and a butter-spattered, frustrated rodent in place of the log and water-soaked lumberjack. After cracking up for a few minutes, we were kind and held the cob to keep it from turning while she ate. As she got older, she got faster and would speed from one plate to the next, snatching her favorite food rather than delicately nibbling as she had when she was young. Finally, we had to lock her up, especially during dessert since cookies, pie and ice cream weren't appropriate food for a squirrel. Not only that, but I drew a line at what I was willing to share, and my dessert was on the wrong side of that line. As I think back to those times, I am reminded of a more recent movie, Ice Age, and Scrat, the saber-tooth squirrel that is so obsessed and possessive of his acorn. Leia could have auditioned for that role.

Between the attachment the kids developed to Leia and her lack of fear of humans or our dogs, there was no way I could release her back to the wild. For the first couple of weeks she was with us, she lived in a hamster cage in the house. I then moved her to an oversized cage – former home of our pet crow, Poe, on the back patio. When we concluded she would remain with the family indefinitely, we upgraded her quarters significantly. Tom and I converted a rarely-used patio and trellis into a twelve-foot square by ten-foot tall cage by surrounding it with chicken wire. We built Leia a small house and extended the cage a couple of feet beyond the concrete patio so she could burrow in the soil. It meant that theoretically, she could dig her way out, but we weren't creating a jail, but rather a spacious home. She had not shown any inclination to run away, so I wasn't concerned she would try to escape. Even though she had never had any adult squirrels to educate her, instinct took over and she dug herself a very nice burrow. She never exactly invited me in, but I did peek, and Quin reached his little arm in and concluded she wasn't digging an escape tunnel, but had a cozy little den that extended about a foot from the entrance.

There were two ways to access Leia's cage – from Quin's bedroom via a sliding glass door and from the backyard through a door we built when we wired her cage – making it easy and convenient to visit her. Whenever any of us went out onto the porch (into her cage) and called her name, she would always pop out of her burrow and come to us - she was a very social little squirrel. Eventually, after a couple of months, I felt she was totally acclimated to her environment, eating well and generally doing very well for herself, so we opened the door from the porch to the yard. She was free to come and go as she pleased. At first, she would cautiously venture out into the yard, rarely going more than ten or fifteen feet from the door, and would scamper back at the slightest disturbance. Slowly, she extended her range and would stay out foraging in the yard for several hours a day, but could always be found "at home" at night. She remained quite social. If any of us walked outside, she would come racing across the yard, up our leg, and onto our shoulder, chattering away as if she had found a long lost friend – even if we hadn't brought a treat for her. We always kept her supplied with food on the porch, but she became more and more self sufficient and returned much less often to the porch.

She also continued to venture out further, and about a year after she had joined our family, Trudy called, quite distressed, and reported, "Shadow (one of her dogs) bit off Princess Leia's tail, and now she's hiding in the hay bales next to the horse pens. Please come quickly!" I figured it must indeed be Leia, as most wild squirrels are wary enough of dogs to not get caught, but Leia had befriended my dogs, who are trained to not chase or otherwise pick on little critters, or larger ones (such as goats), for that matter.

I hustled over, and as soon as I called out her name, Leia rushed over to me. Sure enough, she was missing the last two inches of her tail, and I had a small streak of blood on my right pant leg and the right side of my shirt where she had scurried up to greet me. I took her home and closed the porch door so she would have to stay in while her tail healed. I examined the end of what remained and applied some antibiotic ointment, but felt certain it would heal fine on its own.

About two weeks later, she climbed up on the wire to have her tummy scratched, as she often did when we walked by, but as I started rubbing I noticed that she had very prominent mammary development. I went into her pen, peeked into her den, and with Quin's help, discovered four baby squirrels. I guess she had found a nice boyfriend while she was out in the world. Well, I don't exactly know if he was nice. She never brought him home to meet her family, but she was a very attentive mother. We fought the temptation to hold and play with the babies – heaven knew we already had more than enough pets, and who knew what a neighbor might drop off anytime now. We let them stay "wild," and when they were a few months old, released them in an undeveloped area where we often saw other ground squirrels.

A very young Princess Leia "helping" a young Allie do her homework.

Princess Leia stayed with us, and we opened her door to the yard soon after her babies were gone. She once again spent a lot of time away from her porch, but came home frequently and was always quick to greet us for several more years, the typical lifespan of a squirrel.

I'd Rather Be Lucky than Good

Veterinarians spend four years in school learning how to diagnose disease (and subsequently treat it) and then spend the rest of their careers trying to perfect the skill. I like to think I have learned those lessons well and exercise them carefully to diagnose and treat my patients, but sometimes, I just luck out. I don't subscribe to the theory, "I'd rather be lucky than good." I expect to be good, but I appreciate any lucky breaks I get.

I'll never forget one of those lucky occasions. My very first x-ray machine had arrived several days earlier, on a Thursday afternoon. I thought it was a fabulous machine, complete with an easily-adjustable head, so in addition to "routine" x-rays on small animals, I could also get radiographs on large animals without having to struggle to get them up on a table. I love new toys and was anxious to "play" with this one, but it was not simply a matter of plugging it in. My office was in the back of the barn, which is reached by going up a steep cement driveway, along a decomposed granite gravel path, making a sharp turn, going up six railroad-tie-steps, through the decomposed granite "waiting room," up two tall steps into the actual office, through a small doorway and down the hall. Oh, and the base unit of the x-ray machine was a three-hundred-pound oil-filled tank. And, the floor where the x-ray was to be installed was not strong enough to support the machine.

The delivery company refused to tackle the route to my office, supporting their stance by noting that the floor where the unit was to be installed was not strong enough. Very discouraged, I reluctantly had them leave the x-ray machine in the garage, and went to work asking, begging, pleading, demanding and badgering Tom to remedy the situation. Early Saturday morning, he poured concrete in the new x-ray room. By Sunday evening, it was set well enough that he and Mikey, with my expert supervision, managed to roll/carry/shove/drag/push the x-ray unit up to the office. In addition to the challenging route they had to take, they had to hold the x-ray tank level so the oil would not spill. They grumbled and groaned a lot (guys tend to do that), but by bedtime, the x-ray machine was completely installed in my office.

I needed to take the new x-ray machine for a test run before I could actually charge clients for using it. Plus, as I mentioned earlier, I love new toys and I was anxious to find an opportunity to "play" with this one. I usually do the training (free work) on one of my own animals or one that belongs to a staff member, but none were in need of radiographic diagnostics. Bummer. As I was lamenting the lack of a suitable patient, Mr. Galapagos arrived with Cassidy, a California land tortoise, for a routine physical examination. Mr. Galapagos, a hunched-over, eighty-something-year-old, bespectacled (horn-rimmed, but not tortoise-shell) gentleman, was a new client, but he had been referred by a good friend, so I asked if he would mind letting

Cassidy be my guinea pig, er I mean privileged first patient to be x-rayed with my new machine. I explained that an x-ray could be an especially beneficial examination tool for a tortoise, since so few of its organs can be palpated. He seemed just okay with the idea until I explained that the x-ray would be free, when he suddenly became as anxious to see what the inside of Cassidy looked like as I was to take the unit on its maiden voyage.

Tortoises are very nice to x-ray because they are easy to keep still, and Cassidy was very accommodating. The machine worked like a charm. As I developed the film, however, I was in for quite a surprise. Clearly visible in Cassidy's bladder was a large, round stone. Bladder stones can cause serious problems in a tortoise. Unfortunately, by the time symptoms are evident, it is often too late for a cure. Both Cassidy and I were lucky that day. If I hadn't needed to test drive my new x-ray machine, who knows when I would have made the diagnosis on Cassidy. The subsequent surgery to remove the stone was a success and Cassidy never experienced stone-related symptoms.

She's Mine, All Mine

Sarah, my spider monkey, was two years old when I started dating Tom. She liked him, largely I think because he would roughhouse with her. I frowned on such practice and had never roughhoused with her myself, nor had I let anyone else, because I did not want her to get that first taste of human blood, lest she become addicted. Just kidding! But my reason was not far removed. I didn't want her to think it was OK to bite or chew on human flesh.

So why did I relent with Tom? Why do you think? I was in my mid-twenties, single, and was desperate to get married. Just kidding again! But also not that far from the truth. I enjoyed his company and was very pleased at how good he was with animals, leaving me very interested in pursuing a relationship with him and unwilling to be strict. Sarah benefited from my lapse in judgment – I'll leave it to the reader to determine which aspect of my judgment I'm referring to – because she got to play rough and she loved Tom because of it.

Sarah's love for Tom had limits. She remained very possessive of me and did not allow any body contact between me and any other people. That meant she did not want any hugging or kissing between Tom and me. My dad would have been proud of her. Sarah, of course, was allowed to touch and hug me all she wanted. In spite of her best chaperoning efforts, Tom and I did get married and a year and a half later Allie was born. Sarah didn't mind the immobile infant at all, but as soon as Allie started crawling, Sarah thought of her as either competition or a play-toy – one that she did not particularly like. OK, she despised her. Fortunately, Allie got smart pretty quickly and learned to stay out of reach of Sarah's long arms and tail.

Two years later, Quin was born. He was very interested in the monkey and was slow to learn to stay out of her reach. One day when he was about a year old, I heard him crying loudly and found him out beside Sarah's cage. She had pulled him close, was holding him up next to the cage and was scratching his face. I separated them and took Quin inside to clean his face and calm him down. As it hit me how seriously Sarah could have hurt Quin, I realized that I could no longer keep her. Sarah would have to be euthanized. I could not risk injuring my child.

I put Quin and Allie down for naps and then I went back out to see Sarah. I went inside her cage to have a last visit, determined, but already weeping. She seemed to sense that I was distressed. She quietly crawled up inside my sweatshirt and stuck her head out the neck hole with my head and hugged me. I melted. I couldn't euthanize her. She was just acting like a monkey. She was jealous of my children. She didn't want to share me with anyone else. How could I not respect her perspective and actually appreciate her dedication to me?

Just the same, I had to protect my kids from her. I couldn't expect her to change her behavior, so I enclosed the bottom half of her cage in fine-mesh chicken wire that she could not reach her arms through. She could still reach through the wire on the upper half of the cage, so she could still reach me and any other adults who were allowed to be close to her cage. But all children were now safe from her jealous behavior, and there were no further incidents.

Playtime is Over

Adding a new dog to a household can sometimes be a hassle. Sure, they're amazingly cute and playful and have puppy breath, but their razor-sharp teeth are either aimed at your hands, feet, nose, some other part of your body or your favorite pair of shoes. They make a mess when they eat, and they make the other kind of mess, usually in the house, after they eat. If they weren't so incredibly adorable, you'd wring their little necks.

A nice, mature, older dog can make the introduction much easier. They help teach the little monster the rules of the house, saving you some of the hassle. They also take on the role of puppy sitter, saving you some of the puncture wounds. Osa, ten years old at the time, was definitely a nice and mature older dog when we got Pockey, an eight-week-old Australian Dingo. Her name was three-year-old Allie's pronunciation of "puppy." I had several dogs before Pockey and had seen many more in my vet practice, but Pockey was more energetic than any other dog I had ever seen. She never seemed to stop. She was a tan and white blur of tail and teeth and constantly demonstrated her connections to the Australian outback where her parents had been extracted from wild dens. She seemed to always be coming up with new ways to cause trouble, and she loved to wrestle with Osa, whom she quickly adopted as her long lost, big sister.

Osa was very tolerant most of the time, but Pockey never seemed to tire of playing. I believe in letting animals sort out their hierarchy. Similar to children, there may be momentary screaming and crying, but they do much better than adult humans at working through conflict. Even when there is a lot of snarling and wrestling, there is almost never any bloodshed or injury before the spat is resolved, the pecking order is established, and they are back to playing together. They don't seem to hold grudges like we do.

One day Pockey must not have gotten Osa's subtle hints that she had had enough (actually, she never did) as I heard Osa discipline her so firmly – a loud, aggressive couple of barks and growls – that Pockey screamed for what seemed like minutes. I went to investigate, not by any means mad at Osa, but thinking I might have to suture some wounds this time. But when I checked Pockey over, not only was there no blood, there wasn't even a mark on her. Whatever Osa had said and/or done really worked. Pockey must have left her alone for almost fifteen minutes – an eternity based on her clock – before she was back trying to get her big sister to play. Ah, the joy of a short memory. Something to look forward to as senior moments become more frequent.

Pockey looking in the kitchen window from the pass-through shelf, having bounded up there effortlessly. She would also stand under the orange trees, pop up - also effortlessly - and snatch low-hanging fruit.

Gulp

Rhonda Morgan called early Monday morning to make an appointment for Bruno, her two-year-old Bulldog. She was a bit embarrassed as she started to tell me about the problem. Sunday, after church, Rhonda's husband, Wayne, had been playing with Bruno and had been throwing a Super Ball for him to chase. Bruno would play that game all day long. He loved to chase or to catch the ball, and Wayne and Rhonda loved to watch him skitter, careen and skid around the tiled kitchen. Wayne threw the ball high in the air and Bruno jumped up to catch it. (I have difficulty picturing a Bulldog actually jumping.) Bruno then sat down and looked surprised, but he didn't bring the ball back to Wayne. They thought Bruno had caught the ball, but figured it must have gone under a cabinet or behind the refrigerator. A thorough search failed to find the ball, and they worried slightly that he might have swallowed it, but he acted fine and ate a good dinner, so they figured it had rolled out of sight.

Monday morning Bruno ate a good breakfast, but he immediately vomited the entire meal onto the kitchen floor. This was not normal for Bruno, and Wayne and Rhonda's worry about the missing ball returned. Rhonda called into work, warned them she would be in late, and brought Bruno in to my clinic. The first thing I did was take an x-ray of Bruno's stomach, and there was the Super Ball. Super Balls are small balls made of hard rubber but they tend to swell considerably when immersed in liquid (i.e., a dog's stomach). If he hadn't vomited the ball up with his breakfast, then it was unlikely that he would be able to cough it up later. Nor would it successfully pass in the other direction as it was too big to go through the entire intestinal tract without causing a complete obstruction. We decided that the ball had to be removed surgically.

First thing Tuesday morning, I anesthetized Bruno and prepped him for abdominal surgery. After making my incision, I could palpate the stomach and feel that the ball was still there. I pulled the stomach out through the incision and laid it on the sterile drape surrounding the incision. I made another very small incision into his stomach and squeezed the ball out. I didn't want to risk infection by touching the ball with my hands or by letting it contact anything on the inside of Bruno, so I made sure to aim it over the side of the table. The ball bounced on the ground once and Jenny, who was monitoring Bruno's vital signs, grabbed it before it bounced again. What a catch! Bruno recovered well, and the Morgans switched to larger toys.

Blurry Furballs

Twitchy was a little brown female rabbit that lived with Sean and Tobin, my two prized Pygmy goat bucks. The three shared a chain link pen in my backyard. I did provide for Twitchy's dignity, giving her a rabbit house (a small dog house) filled with old towels into which she could burrow. In spite of her spiffy digs and her handsome pen-mates, Twitchy was an accomplished escape artist. She would regularly break out of not just the pen, but also the entire backyard. Occasionally I caught her outside the pen but still inside the yard. If not, I usually found her escape route – it's remarkable how little space a rabbit needs to squeeze under a fence – but I learned to not close the route off until she returned, which she invariably did within a week or two. I guess even rabbits realize you just can't beat the free meals and other comforts of home.

On a cold, very rainy morning – there's no such thing as a warm, rainy morning in Southern California, at least as far as I'm concerned – I went out to feed Twitchy, Sean and Tobin, and to my horror, the lower half of the pen was littered with hunks of wet brown fur. "Damn," I thought, "a coyote must have gotten into the pen and eaten Twitchy." I was just sick, thinking of the horrible death she must have suffered. A little relief bubbled up as I recognized that the goats were unharmed. The brief respite was quickly replaced by anger at the mayhem that coyotes can cause.

After throwing a flake of hay into the goat's feeder, with tears of sadness and frustration mixing with the steady rain and my naturally poor eyesight, I bent down to pick up a piece of the fur. When the clump squirmed in my hand, I nearly dropped it in surprise. To my delight, it wasn't just a mangy wad of hair; it was a live furball, a very wet baby bunny! I picked up a total of seven of these little hunks of wet brown fur and stuffed them in my jacket pockets. Once they were dry, they turned into soft, cuddly baby bunnies! Apparently the wooden rabbit house was not up to her standards, and Twitchy's digging was not restricted to getting out of her pens. She had also dug a long tunnel to create a warren for her new family, and they been washed out by the torrential rain. Her excursions outside the yard must have included some romance since I didn't have a "daddy" rabbit in the yard. I gathered up Mama along with the babies and set up the whole crew in a large, dry pen in the garage. I was now in the unique position of pawning baby bunnies off on neighbors and friends, paying them back for all the animals they had dumped on me over the years.

Dog Band-Aid

Allie and Quin went to preschool with Gary and Travis Hale. Gary and Travis's mom, Briana, and I met in the parking lot early in the school year while waiting for our kids. We became best friends almost immediately, and we still are today. Besides sometimes taking turns dropping off and picking up the kids, we also listed one another on the emergency call list at the school.

It was in the spring when sure enough, I got a call from Mrs. Bryant, the director of the preschool. She couldn't reach Briana – this was before the age of cell phones – but Gary had burned his finger and wanted to go home. I left a message on Briana's answering machine and made the short drive to the school. The students had been "helping" the teacher prepare a mid-morning snack of chicken and stars soup and crackers. Gary, only 4 years old at the time, was pulling himself up so he could peek in the pot and had touched his index finger on the electric stove. The physical wound was a small blister, and Mrs. Bryant had administered the proper first aid – burn ointment and a Band-Aid – but Gary was still upset and wanted to go home. He remained rather upset when it was I, rather than his mother, who came to pick him up.

I knew Briana wouldn't be home for at least an hour, and Gary was clearly going to make it a very long hour, so I decided to try some child psychology. I spent the drive home sympathizing with Gary about the severity of his injury, marveling at the strength and bravery he was demonstrating in the face of such a severe wound. Hey, not only had I been raising two kids of my own, but I had been married for five years, so I had learned to play to the male's machismo.

I had only made grudging progress in soothing the wounded chef in the car, so when we got home, I suggested we go up to my clinic and put a real dog bandage on his injured finger. Now I was starting to make some real progress! Gary thought that was an excellent idea. First we removed his Band-Aid. I combined all my medical and maternal skills to create an overwhelming aura of concern and professionalism. I carefully examined his finger and agreed with him that it was indeed a serious injury. I applied a fresh dose of burn ointment and then wrapped his finger with far more than the required amount gauze and tape. The bandage was three times as large as his finger and it certainly drew attention to the fact that he had an injury. The pain was almost completely eliminated – but I knew it was the "mental quality" of the bandage and not my ointment. By the time his mother arrived, Gary was enthralled with his bandage and thrilled to show it off. I think it was days before Briana was allowed to remove it so Gary could take a proper bath!

Am I Glad to See You!

It was a dark and stormy night. Well, it wasn't really stormy. It was a chilly autumn evening, but fellow Snoopy fans will recognize the line. Anyway, on this particular dark and stormy night, as Tom, the kids and I were finishing dinner, the ever-calm and sedate Osa abandoned her spot at our feet (waiting for food to drop to the floor), stood alert by the sliding door, and started barking at something, or someone, in the backyard. Tom and the kids barely raised their heads from their dinner plates, but I followed Osa out into the backyard to see what had put her on high alert. Note that I said I followed her, not the reverse. I don't watch or like horror flicks, but I know enough about them to not storm, or even wander, out into the dark to investigate creepy sounds. Oh, yes, I also turned on the patio lights before venturing out, which ended up providing a comic aspect to the event, as one of the lights almost perfectly framed Sarah the monkey hugging the back side of the house like a cat burglar. She reminded me of a criminal or escaped prisoner, frozen in place, caught in the glare of the spotlight. She quickly broke free of the trance when she saw me. She raced over and climbed up into my arms, hugging me tightly.

She had escaped from her cage that was around the side and toward the front of the house, but was becoming more and more frightened as she moved away from the safety of her home. She was obviously thrilled to see me, and she chattered away as I hugged and cuddled and reassured her. She was probably telling me about all the scary and dangerous things she had imagined out there in the wild.

Sarah didn't like Allie or Quin, but she loved Pockey. Here, she is grooming her furry friend.

I carried her inside and held her – well, it was more her clinging to me – as I finished my dessert, a scrumptious slice of chocolate pie with whipped cream topping. I was anxious to figure out how Sarah had escaped, but I didn't trust two young kids and their sometimes devilish father to restrain themselves from divvying up my portion of the pie. As protective as I am of my sweets, I did share a bite with my traumatized monkey. Once I had finished savoring that delicious treat – it was I, after all, that had baked it – I carried Sarah out and put her back into her cage. She was quite content to return to the familiar, comfortable surroundings, but immediately reached through the wires to hug me. I disengaged myself from her grasp, walked several paces away and called to her. Lucky for me, Sarah wasn't as sneaky or calculating as Kippy had been when he stored up leash so he could attack Dad. She immediately went to a corner of the cage, pushed the wire away from the wood frame, slipped out, and bounded over to me and back up into my arms. Good monkey. I never would have noticed the loose wire or the missing staples if she had not shown me where to look.

Dinner – and dessert – being over, Tom and the kids had followed us outside, so I kept Sarah in my arms while Tom fetched a hammer and fresh staples and sealed her escape hatch. I felt extremely lucky that I was home when she escaped. I had nightmares for weeks thinking of all the horrible things that could have happened if I hadn't been there.

Fly Away Crow

Years later, after Edgar Allen Poe the Crow had gone to the great hay bale treasure trove in the sky, Geraldine Snyder found an injured adult crow in her yard. This was before the days of West Nile Virus, so she had no reason to fear her. She gathered the crow up in a towel and brought her to me, "the local animal rescue and refuge facility." She was a mature crow and had a large open wound high up on her leg. She had probably lost an argument with a dog and was lucky to have escaped with such a minor injury. She did, however, need treatment or the wound would become infected and she would ultimately lose the argument permanently.

Tom, my ever-witty husband, named the bird LBJ, not after Lyndon Baines Johnson, the thirty-sixth President of the United States, but rather after his wife, Lady Bird. I anesthetized LBJ and sutured her wound. It looked like it would heal very nicely. I put her in an outside flight cage for several weeks so I could keep her on antibiotics and give the wound time to heal. Our homemade chicken wire flight cage was so named because it was about six feet long by three feet wide and four feet tall.

Not huge, but large enough for a crow to fully expand its wings and flutter around some. My plan was to make an opening in the top of the cage for her to fly out of when she was ready.

Accommodating such a large cage was not too difficult, thanks to our large yard and the many concrete patios off the back of the house. LBJ's cage was on the patio off the family room, adjacent to the kitchen. One of the many great features of our house was its large kitchen with a long window above the sink and adjacent counters. It looked out on the patio and backyard with its large pepper and orange trees and rolling hills in the distant background. I always enjoyed the view, but not enough to do dishes by hand in place of using the dishwasher. One morning, while loading the dishwasher with breakfast dishes, I looked out on the patio and saw another crow hopping around on the ground beside the cage. It was visiting LBJ, providing an opportunity I couldn't pass up. I hurriedly, but somewhat cautiously, went out the sliding glass door from the family room to the patio. Fortunately, crows are rather brash, so LBJ's visitor fluttered a short distance away, but didn't fly off. I opened the door to LBJ's cage and let her join her friend. They took off and I figured I'd seen the last of her. I had not planned on making the opening in her cage for another week, but decided she had the best chance of doing well in the company of a healthy companion.

Several months later, I was in the front yard fighting a losing battle with the weeds when Susie Hatcher walked up my driveway with a young baby crow that she had found on the ground beside her horse corral. I love my work and love animals, but I admit that I thought something like, "Aaargh! I just got rid of one of those.

Won't you people please quit dumping animals on me!" It was only a thought, and a brief one at that.

Susie lived about a quarter of a mile down the street. She had walked from her corral to my house with the baby crow. The bird looked fine and tried to fly, but couldn't stay airborne long enough to fly away. Apparently he had flunked his first flight lesson. I promised I would feed him for a short while and then release him. As Susie was about to leave, she casually mentioned that two other crows seemed to be very interested in the fledgling and had been dive-bombing her while she carried her to my house. I looked up and saw two adult crows circling above us, and you guessed it, one of them was LBJ, my somewhat recent patient! She was easy to identify because her tail feathers were still deformed from being in the somewhat cramped quarters of the flight cage for over a month.

My earlier frustration at being treated as the local rescue station evaporated. I was elated to know that LBJ had not just survived, but thrived back in the real world, enough so to be raising her own chick. I put the fledgling in the same flight cage his mother had occupied and kept him there for a week. The cage served two purposes – to protect him from predators and to allow him to mature sufficiently before he took his next flying lesson. LBJ and her husband checked on him regularly during the time we kept him. At the end of the week, when I saw them circling above, I went out and opened the top of the cage. The fledgling passed this flight test with flying colors, spiraled his way up to his parents, and the three of them flew off together.

What a Deer Family

Over the years of working with zoos and amusement parks, I always preferred working on the animals early in the morning before the general public had access to the area. I didn't do dastardly, devilish and ghoulish things that had to be hidden from the public, but I could concentrate on my examination or treatment rather than worry about the impression we were making on the visitors. Sometimes the early work was mandatory. If we had to use a tranquilizer dart to do a knock-down on an animal, I didn't want to take the chance that an errant shot resulted in the knock-down of an unsuspecting visitor rather than the target animal. While it might generate lots of free publicity for the park or zoo, it's probably not the kind of P.R. the facility (or I) would really want.

Late one toasty mid-July afternoon, I was called to a local park to serve as midwife for a Fallow deer. Falline, a beautiful deep tan doe with a white chest, had been in labor for several hours. She had pushed out an amniotic bubble, but she had not presented any part of the fawn. It was time to help her out.

Falline was housed in a pen with Nelson, a massive buck with a large rack of antlers who happened to be her husband. I am not a hunter, nor do I support hunting, but I suspect that any park visitors that were hunters looked at Nelson and dreamed of bagging him out in the wild. Now, as many parents can appreciate, it was not the mother-to-be that needed to be calmed, but the expectant father. The facility did not have a separate holding pen or any other way to physically separate the two. Their enclosure was, however, a long, narrow pen, so I decided to herd Falline into one end and Nelson into the other. Nelson nervously "agreed" to go to the other end, but in the process charged past me. Although his body wasn't even close to me, that beautiful large rack of his extended way out and the end of his antler caught me across the right side of my face, sending me crashing into the side of the pen. Fortunately, I wasn't knocked unconscious, and more amazingly I didn't pass out. I would, however, end up with quite a shiner.

In addition to not being able to completely separate Falline from Nelson, we could not take her "off exhibit," that is, separate her from the many people who were visiting that day. There was a huge crowd of people and they were all anxious to watch the delivery. The keepers caught Falline and held her in the corner. I cleaned my hand and arm well, lubricated them, and reached in to see what was going on inside. The fawn's head was turned back, but I was able to straighten it out into a normal delivery position. While I was rearranging the fawn's head, I could only think of the distress of the crowd of people if it was already dead. So I cheated. I put my finger into the fawn's mouth. I felt the little tongue move and knew that we were headed for a happy ending. I started pulling on the feet to deliver the fawn and she slowly made her appearance. She was alive and well and the "show" was a success. We did rope off the pen then to keep the visitors away and put up shade-cloth to give mom and baby some privacy while they got acquainted. All went well, and the whole family happily performed for the public the next day. My black eye, on the other hand, took a couple of weeks to heal.

I'm Sorry. I Had No Idea

When Osa was twelve years old, her face had grayed somewhat, especially below her mouth, she was nearly deaf – although she could always hear food drop into her bowl or onto the floor – and she didn't see very well either. Her looks, vision and hearing may have faded, but her love of little creatures, which started with Peanut, my parents' teacup poodle, never wavered. She had even had her own pet rabbit that she named "Ruff."

By the time Osa was twelve, Ruff had gone on to the rabbit warren in the sky, but we still had plenty of other critters in our menagerie, including a pair of ducks named Donald and Daisy. They had the run of the backyard, just as Osa did. Osa and the ducks coexisted peacefully. She would sometimes follow them around the yard, and sometimes they would follow her. They certainly weren't afraid of her. Come to think of it, I never did notice an animal that acted fearful of Osa, in spite of her size. Well, with the exception of Coquette, that is.

Osa's interest in ducks increased markedly when Donald and Daisy had a clutch of eighteen ducklings. The proud parents took their not-so-little family on regular tours of the yard. It was very cute to watch. It went from cute to almost hilarious when their nineteenth child would join the procession – Osa. Anytime she was out and the family would go for a walk, she would trail behind them, fascinated by all the little ducklings. I never bred Osa, but her maternal instincts were world class.

On a typically gorgeous summer afternoon, I was on the patio soaking up the sun while watering plants. I was also watching Osa gently lick a ducklet, who seemed quite content with the special attention he was getting. As I was enjoying the show, a loud, very discontent peeping started, but it wasn't from the ducklet that was being bathed. Poor Osa was inadvertently standing on another baby duck and couldn't hear its cries of distress! I raced over to them and gave Osa a quick slap on the side and moved her off the baby. The ducklet was fine and ran off to momma Daisy. Osa, on the other hand, was shattered. She had no idea that she had been doing anything wrong. She was just loving on a baby duck and yet I had just punished her. I spent the rest of the afternoon apologizing to her. Boy, did I love that dog! Still do.

I Told You I Didn't Want to Watch

Misery loves company and it was nice to know that I was not the only one who had a propensity to sink to the ground in a dead faint at inopportune times. One of my clients, Annabelle Marini, a thirty-something year-old hairdresser (my hairdresser) with striking green eyes and gorgeous, long raven hair, had a tendency to pass out whenever she saw one of her beloved animals being treated. She had several pets, including three dogs, a pair of sheep, and one goat, that were my patients. It didn't take us long to realize that Annabelle was better off staying in the waiting area while my staff and I took care of her animals. Even observing a simple injection was enough to send her slumping to the floor. Once her animals were treated and back home, she could take care of them without difficulty, even irrigating punctures and changing bandages on open, bloody wounds. There was just something about being there when the deed was done, so to speak. Or at least that's what I thought – until the day I dehorned her recently-adopted goat Randy, a relatively small, chocolate-colored, adult Nubian wether.

With his floppy, cream-colored ears, Randy was cute, but by breeding standards, he didn't measure up. That's why Annabelle had come to adopt him. Unlike his previous owners, who only wanted the finest according to the breeding standard, Annabelle was only concerned about personality, and Randy had that in spades. Even though he was friendly and docile, a wether's horns are a nuisance at best and can inflict severe, even if accidental, pain. Show goats are not allowed to have horns, and pets are far safer without their horns too. I'm not sure why his original owners had not had him dehorned, but Annabelle chose to make sure he was a safe pet.

She dropped Randy off just after lunch, making plans to pick him up later that day. So far, so good. She wouldn't even be in the waiting room, so she was in no danger of fainting on us. Randy's horns were quite large; large enough that I had to saw them off (only very young goats can be "disbudded," which is a more minor procedure). First, I gave him a heavy tranquilizer and then shaved an area around each horn to help prevent an infection. I injected a local anesthetic to numb the horns and the area around them. After sawing off the horns and cauterizing the wounds, I packed a small amount of cotton into the small holes that remained – all standard procedure, no unexpected occurrences. With the surgery complete, we put Randy in a small stall to finish recovering from his tranquilizer. Fifteen or twenty minutes later, as we were treating an abscess on an ancient Himalayan cat, we could tell that the tranquilizer had fully worn off, as Randy was noisily expressing his discontent at the indignities I had put him through – always a good sign in an animal coming out of an anesthetic.

Annabelle arrived just before closing time, paid her bill, and I went with her to fetch Randy from his stall. One look at the top of his head with a large shaved area and the wads of slightly-reddened cotton sticking out where his horns used to be and Annabelle promptly collapsed. Luckily, I was standing right behind her and was able to ease her to the ground, saving her from cracking her skull on the railing of the adjacent stall or the cement floor in that area. Annabelle's face quickly went from sickly white to flaming red as she came to and realized what had happened. She had a hard time living that incident down, but she always reminded me that she had learned from a pro!

That Mockingbird Won't Go

Spring is a tough season for baby birds. It is not uncommon to find a baby bird on the ground – often up close to a wall or the base of a tree. Some babies are knocked out of the nest by winds (remember the Mother Goose nursery rhyme Rock-a-Bye Baby?) or other creatures (who probably intended to eat the baby but dropped it by accident). Other babies flunk their first flying lesson and end up on the ground, unable to fly back up to their nest. Unfortunately, the parent birds can't pick up the baby and carry it back either. They will continue to take care of it on the ground but local cats and dogs will usually "take care of it" before it learns to fly.

Let me digress momentarily to dispel an old wives' tale. If you find a baby bird, ideally you should put it back into its nest. Contrary to what you've likely heard, the mother will still take care of the baby even if human hands have touched it. If you can't reach the nest, put the baby in a deep basket – a stand-in for its nest – and hang the basket close to the original nest. If you can't see the nest, assume it is nearby, and hang the basket accordingly. This will protect it from ground-based predators. Mom and dad bird will find the baby and will continue to care for it.

The preceding lesson was prompted by the following story and several similar ones. Marilyn Jennings found a baby mockingbird in her yard. She couldn't find the nest, didn't see the parents, and hadn't read this book, so she brought the bird to me. The baby must have been blown or knocked out his nest, because he was way too young to have been trying to fly. He was just beginning to get his feathers. Of course, I agreed to care for the little guy, which I'm sure is what Marilyn had anticipated. A baby mockingbird "gapes" when its mom or dad lands on the nest to offer food. It opens its mouth, which has yellow "lips," wide and screams for food. Mom uses the yellow ring around the mouth as if it was a basketball goal, does an impression of Shaquille O'Neal, and stuffs food down its baby's little throat. Chirper (it seemed like a good name for a noisy little bird) quickly accepted me as his new "mom" and would gape and scream whenever I came near. I would do my

part and stuff the appropriate foods down his throat –
just like his real mom. I must admit, though, that I
didn't totally emulate his mother; I didn't hold the
worms in my mouth when I offered them to him. Yuck!

I must have been a good "cook" because he grew well,
and in a few weeks his feathers had filled in completely
and he was ready to fly. Now came another situation
where I was not only unwilling but unable to emulate
his mother. Chirper didn't know how to fly and had
nobody to teach him. I had my private pilot's license,
but I don't think my type of flight training would have
benefited him. I don't think he really even knew he was
a bird. He had imprinted on me, so he really thought he
was a small human, and he thoroughly enjoyed walking
around on the dinner table while we ate. Figuring he
could never develop into a full-fledged member of our
human family, I started the "weaning" or reintroduction
process by putting his cage out on the porch during the
day so the other mockingbirds could come visit - and
they actually did! After a few days of regular visitors
separated by the jail (cage) bars, I opened his cage door,
giving him the option to come and go.

By this time he was eating on his own and I kept his
dish full. For several days, he would flutter out of his
cage and down to the ground, then hop into a nearby
bush where he'd spend most of the day. Each evening at
dinnertime, I would go outside, whistle and call out,
"Chirper!" He usually answered from a low spot in a
bush, from where I would pick him up and put him back
in his cage, and he would spend the night in the house.
One evening I called and his answering call came from
high up in a pepper tree. He must be learning to fly! I
left him out alone for the first time, almost as worried as
when my children boarded the bus for the first day of

school, fervently hoping he had made friends with some of the other mockingbirds and that he would stay up high, away from the cats, raccoons, opossums, and other predators in our area.

Chirper never came inside again, but I did keep food in his cage for another week – just in case he was having trouble finding his own. He continued to answer my calls each evening for several weeks, so I knew he was alive which meant he must be finding enough food, as his dish went untouched for many days. It gave me a good feeling to know I had helped him to survive and I was especially happy that he was out on his own and hadn't needed to spend the rest of his life in a cage. Marilyn had kept track of her foundling's progress, stopping by to visit a few times, so she shared the warm feelings.

Rockets Red Glare

The morning after Orange Park Acres' big Fourth of July celebration, which included a spectacular fireworks display launched from the local golf and tennis club, I was up early as usual and headed out front to feed all the animals. As soon as the garage door started opening, Sarah, the spider monkey, started chattering, Bam, the horse, started whinnying, and all the Pygmy goats started bleating, urging me to hurry up with their breakfast. It was my standard morning greeting, and I loved it. On this morning, I had an additional, unexpected visitor greeting me.

My first stop was just outside the garage to feed Sarah. She chattered excitedly in anticipation of her daily grapes, raisin bread (she picked out all the raisins and ate them before eating any of the bread), monkey biscuits and assorted other items. After Sarah, the next stop was the barn to get a flake of hay for Bam. As I approached the gate to the barn, which also served as the entrance to my clinic, an interloper sat up and started wagging his whip-like black tail furiously while his tongue lolled out of his mouth flapping back and forth almost in sync with his tail. I immediately recognized the stocky six-year-old, black and white Pit Bull as a patient, the lovable and loving Hoss. But he didn't belong here. He had been to the clinic about a week earlier for his annual vaccinations, but his family, Anna and Lester Thomas and their three kids, lived nearly a mile away, on the other side of a major street.

Hoss gave me no choice but to stop and greet him, showing his affection and appreciation by slathering me with his monstrous tongue. I checked him over quickly and didn't find any wounds. He seemed perfectly healthy, so I mollified Bam with his hay and continued on to feed the impatient herd of Pygmy goats in the back of the barn. With the resident animals happily immersed in their meals, I opened up the office, looked up the Thomas' phone number and gave them a call. Anna answered the phone, and I could feel as well as hear her sigh of relief over the phone. They had discovered that Hoss was missing the night before – it was pretty obvious as you'll read below – and had spent hours walking and driving around the neighborhood in search of their lost companion.

Hoss was large for a Pit Bull, weighing about ninety pounds, and like most of his breed, he was incredibly strong and powerful. He was, however, as kind and gentle as a Labrador Retriever. A lover, not a fighter, he got along marvelously with his humans and the other dogs and cats in the family. Hoss had one weakness, though, one shared by many dogs, children, and a few adults, for that matter – a numbing fear of thunderstorms and other loud noises, including it seems, fireworks.

Anna, Lester and the kids had been at the same fireworks show I had attended with my family. Aware of his fear of loud noises, they had brought Hoss in from his normal nighttime spot in his outside doghouse and locked him in the garage. When they returned late in the evening and turned into the driveway, they could plainly see something was wrong with the garage door. It was askew and there was a ragged, gaping hole in the lower right side. While they were worried about Hoss, their first assumption was that someone had broken into the house through the garage. They decided to try the automatic garage door opener, figuring there wasn't much to lose and thinking it would scare off anybody that was still in the house. The door opener worked, but they found the door to the house still locked and nothing was disturbed or missing in the house.

When they went back to look for Hoss, they inspected the damage to the garage door more carefully and discovered scratch marks and bite marks. They realized the damage wasn't due to somebody trying to get into the garage, but rather it was due to Hoss successfully getting out of the garage. He had literally chewed through the garage door and taken off. Apparently the sound of the fireworks had penetrated the garage walls. Combined with the flashing lights that appeared through the garage windows, it had all been too much for Hoss.

Exactly how, or for that matter why, Hoss made it to my clinic, we'll never know, but I was sure glad he considered my clinic a safe place to seek refuge. As we puzzled over why he ended up at my place, Anna quipped, "I guess he wanted some tranquilizers."

Repeat Performance - Plus

My work with goats and sheep led, in the mid-seventies, to a fascination with Pygmy goats. As the name implies, Pygmy goats are smaller than other breeds, such as Alpine, Nubian and Saanen, and are therefore primarily kept as pets and for exhibition, rather than for their milk. I started with one, Gabby, as a pet. My "fascination" led not to one or two as pets, but an entire breeding herd of up to twenty goats (more when the does were kidding). Breeding and showing the adults and selling the kids became a sideline business, which I named Quillie Acres Pygmy Goats. Fascination grew to obsession and led all the way to me being the president of the National Pygmy Goat Association (NPGA).

As with all breeding programs, I would introduce new bloodlines by bringing outside bucks in to work as stud and sometimes by buying a doe from another breeder. I purchased Midnight as an adult goat. As her name implies, Midnight was jet black. While many Pygmy goats are largely all black, the goats that I had seen before had at least white crowns and ears. Another characteristic of Pygmy goats, and of all goats for that matter, is they usually have one or two kids at a time.

121

Midnight proved her uniqueness the first time I bred her and she had quadruplets. All four babies did well and I found homes for all of them. I bred her again but ended up selling her part way through her pregnancy.

"Midnight delivered quads the last time she was pregnant." I warned the new owner, Mr. Kaspar. "And as fat as she is this time, there's a chance she might have quads again." This caused no undue stress to Mr. Kaspar; in fact he was looking forward to the possibility of having multiple kids. He was just starting his own goat farm, so the instant growth in herd size would be a boon. Shortly after her due date, my curiosity was bubbling over, so I called Mr. Kaspar to see how Midnight was doing. "Any chance she delivered quadruplets again?" I asked. "No," he replied happily, "this time she had six kids!" All of them did fine, and Mr. Kaspar was thrilled. What a way to start a herd in one fell swoop!

Priorities Out of Order

Animals rate at different levels in different households. Some of us hold our animals in equal or higher esteem than our human friends and relations. Others, sadly, treat their pets and livestock as if they were an inconvenience at best. As wonderfully amazed as I have been by the magical and inspiring things I've seen and heard of animals doing, I have been doubly shocked, appalled, dismayed and often darn-right ticked off at what some of their owners have done.

One case in point, certainly not the most egregious one, occurred naturally on a windy, rainy Saturday. I received a call from Sandy Turner, who reported that she had a three-year-old Hampshire ewe that was having trouble delivering. Sandy wasn't sure when the ewe had gone into labor, but this morning she had noticed a tail hanging out of her vulva, and the ewe was lethargic. I suggested that she bring the ewe to me as soon as possible (as in *immediately*).

Allie and Quin, seven and five-years old at the time, had just finished cleaning the living room and clearing space for the Christmas tree we were preparing to go pick out. They apparently anticipated getting a very large tree or a horde of presents – probably both – because they had cleared a huge area. They were practically bouncing off the walls with anticipation of our trip to the Christmas tree lot, but there was no doubt that this ewe needed my help. Fortunately, they were (and still are) very good and understanding children, so although clearly crestfallen, they accepted my promise that I wouldn't be too long and that we would make gingerbread cookies in the afternoon, and went to review their Christmas wish lists while I got ready for the Turners.

Sandy, a petite strawberry-blonde in her early thirties and her contrastingly tall and burly husband Jerry pulled up towing a horse trailer. The ewe was lying on the metal floor of the trailer – no blanket, not even any straw – and she was obviously exhausted. When I examined her, there truly was a tail hanging out her vulva, and she was too tired to even stand up. I already had a bucket of warm water and some lubricant, so I washed up and reached inside her to check on the position of the lamb. As indicated by the exposed tail, it was in a breech presentation, and unsurprisingly the lamb was dead. She must have been trying to deliver this lamb for many hours. Her tissues were swollen and the lamb was completely dry. All natural lubrication was gone. I got the lamb turned and repositioned into a natural posterior presentation. Even after lubricating my arms and as much of the ewe and lamb as I could reach, for the first, and so far the only, time in my veterinary career, I had to sit down on the ground, put a foot up on the ewe's rear end, grab the feet of the lamb and pull. I got the dead lamb out, but both the ewe and I were beat.

Allie and Quin had come out to watch, and soon after I had managed to extract the lamb, Allie, squeezing her nose in disgust, squeaked, "Oh man, it smells like a garbage can, Mom." She was right, and her tone mimicked my attitude of disgust. The lamb had been dead in the womb so long that it had begun to rot. I put the ewe on antibiotics, and she did fine, although I don't know if she ever got pregnant again.

The length of time the ewe must have been in labor without her owners noticing is at least terribly regrettable and I feel criminally negligible. I admit that even in the best and most carefully monitored situations, not all ewes are well lubricated and not all lambs are delivered alive. Just the same, you may better appreciate my vitriol when I share what I learned during the course of extracting the dead lamb. It turns out that Sandy and Jerry had intended to sail to Catalina Island first thing that morning. They had spent the night on their boat in anticipation of setting sail at first light, but the severe weather prevented the trip and they returned home. Thus, they had time to check on the pregnant ewe and bring her to the vet. I will always wonder if she would even have survived if it had been a nice day and her owners had gone sailing. I also wonder if they had paid just a bit more attention to their pregnant ewe if they might have had a live lamb, too.

I Didn't Used to be Superstitious

I've never really been a superstitious person, so I scheduled a spay on a Friday the 13th. Muffin was an eight-month-old tabby cat in apparent good health. It should have been a routine surgery.

I've always kept my surgical cases a little light on anesthesia, out of respect for its power. As I was completing Muffin's procedure, which had indeed gone smoothly, she started wiggling a little. Rather than give her another dose, which would prolong her recovery, I had Lucy, my assistant, hold her tight while I finished sewing her up. I put in the last suture, removed the drape, and stripped off my gloves. I was about to get up and wash my hands, expecting that Lucy would finish cleaning Muffin and put her in a cage to recover, when instead she said, "She's stopped breathing." Not exactly the update I was looking for. I quickly examined Muffin, but I couldn't detect breathing nor could I pick up a heart beat. I started resuscitation procedures but was unable to get her heart beating again. Damn! I dreaded calling Muffin's owner, and needless to say, she was devastated. I really, really hate losing a patient, especially when there's no good reason, but it hurts just as bad or worse when I have to tell their owner, because then I feel doubly guilty – for losing the patient and the heartache I've dealt to the human. I did become a bit more superstitious, and I try hard not to schedule any surgeries for any Friday the 13th.

Goats, Goats, and More Goats!

Pygmy goats can be very fertile little creatures. Quadruplets and quintuplets are not uncommon. What's the big deal about that? Dogs regularly have eight and sometimes thirteen or more puppies. The problem is that a female dog has nine teats, but a doe only has two teats on her udder. Not nearly enough faucets onto which to "plug" a set of quadruplets. In spite of that anatomical limitation, I have often seen all four quadruplets with their heads in mom's flanks and their tails wagging happily. I've always associated wagging tails with nursing. I have no idea what the second two kids were sucking on! I admit that more than once I inspected mom to make sure I hadn't missed something – like the sudden appearance of two additional teats.

Goats may have a herd mentality, but they're not stupid. I found that many quadruplets and quintuplets were quite crafty, as they learned to steal milk from other nursing mothers. This is not as simple as latching onto a free teat. A mother goat won't let just any kid nurse. She lets her baby start nursing and then turns and sniffs the baby's tail. If it is not her kid, she butts it away and won't let it nurse. If it is her kid, she relaxes, lets down her milk, and starts chewing her cud to pass the time. The quadruplet kids learned to wait until one of mom's legitimate kids started to nurse and mom went into relaxed mode before they would sneak in on the other side and gulp down as much as possible before they were noticed by the other mom and pushed away. I am amazed at how quickly they learned that perfect timing was essential to avoid being sniffed out as an interloper and butted away. Ultimately, it comes from survival instinct (and hunger), so I guess I shouldn't be too surprised.

Oh, That Feels Good

Male dogs have a unique reproductive anatomy. They have a gland on their penis that swells when they are breeding a female. This gland normally swells after the male has penetrated the female and then causes a "tie" which keeps the penis in the female until the swelling goes down. The two dogs are thus held together for five to twenty minutes to maximize the likelihood of achieving a pregnancy. Other than during breeding, this gland is shrunken and not noticeable.

Occasionally, the male dog will become stimulated for non-sexual reasons. The owner may be petting his belly and accidentally rub over the gland and it will begin to swell. The swelling can become quite large and firm. In this instance, however, the penis and the swollen glands are still inside the sheath, so it is not immediately obvious that it is a swollen penis. It looks like it is a swelling just under the skin of the belly, which can appear quite alarming to an untrained observer.

One Sunday afternoon, while I was working on stained glass at home, I heard the business line ring (I had an extension in the house). After hours and on weekends, if I was around, I usually monitored the answer machine, in case there was an emergency I could take care of. In my outgoing recording I gave information about emergency clinics, so clients often did not leave a message. When the caller did leave a message, it was usually about routine business or something else that could easily wait until regular clinic hours. There were times, though, that I could pick up the phone and either take care of the problem with a few instructions or step into action and see the animal right then.

On this particular occasion, I literally had my hands full with a large piece of stained glass that I was foiling, but I could hear the incoming message. It was Jenny, one of my very good clients, and she was extremely anxious and concerned. I set down my piece of glass and grabbed the phone. Jenny explained, rather rapidly, that she had been petting Ralph, her four-year-old male chocolate Labrador, and he had suddenly developed a hard swelling between his hind legs. She described how it had grown so suddenly and quickly, and she was convinced it was going to explode. What should she do?! Would I come over to her house, or should she rush him over to my clinic? She seemed to have gotten all that out on a single breath of air. When she paused to breathe, I jumped in because I had a strong suspicion of what the problem was.

I asked a few questions. Had she been stroking his belly? A mildly surprised, "Yes." Is there a chance she may have rubbed his "sensitive area"? A hesitant and slightly embarrassed, "I guess so." Is the swelling just behind there? A dawning, "Indeed it is." At that point, I suggested that an emergency visit wasn't warranted, that Ralph probably just needed a cold shower. A jump into her cold swimming pool would serve the same purpose. She was very embarrassed when I explained what was going on, but over the years, she has been joined by many other men and women with the same question about their dog. The jump in the pool did indeed resolve the swelling.

Bird Brain

When she was ten years old, Allie wanted a pet parakeet. Given my profession and my propensity to "collect" animals, I was in no position to argue. In actuality, I was quite pleased she was developing an affection for animals. After getting her solemn pledge that she would assume complete responsibility for the bird, we went to visit a family friend who raised parakeets. Geri gave us a baby that had just barely come out of the nest box. He was very frightened and sat in the corner of his cage admonishing anyone who came near. Initially, Allie was almost as scared as the scolding little chick, distraught that he didn't take to her immediately. She persevered, though, spending hours each day standing with her hand in the cage, tears running from her eyes. It probably felt like years to Allie, but in just a few days, Claude was her devoted pet and friend. Eventually Allie could open her mouth and Claude would climb part way in and clean her braces.

Starting with those first fearful days, Claude was always a vocal little parakeet. He saved his loudest screams for whenever I held him. That was probably because I usually only held him to trim a chronically cracked toenail. It's standard practice to properly restrain a bird while treating it, so as to keep it from damaging its wings trying to escape and to keep it from biting you. Distressed by Claude's cries, Allie implored "He won't bite you, Mom" and talked me out of restraining him properly. She was right. He never did – lucky for him (and me).

While he remained a noisy bird, he quickly outgrew the fear, becoming rather bold. He was also quite clever. Allie spent hours with her door closed, allowing Claude to explore at will and teaching him several tricks (including the brace-cleaning maneuver). His bravery and craftiness eventually caused him big trouble. He figured out how to open his cage one night and flew down to Allie's bed.

Unbeknownst to poor Claude, Allie was not alone. Panther, my mom's thirteen-year-old, three-legged cat was visiting us for awhile and had chosen Allie's bed as a favorite sleeping spot. Instinctively, Panther grabbed Claude. Although Allie quickly rescued her bird from Panther's clutches, Claude died from an infection two days later. Ironically, Panther died of old age just two weeks later. Claude was the only prey Panther ever caught.

The Bigger They Are

Jim Hansen was a muscular 27-year-old "surfer dude" with stereo-typical wavy, long sandy-blonde hair. Jim, who worked at the local home supply center, always caught the eye of ladies, including my staff, who were quite pleased whenever he would bring in his mom's three-year-old dachshund, Gretel. Mind you, they were never hoping for anything bad to happen to Gretel. They were just pleased when they sent out vaccination reminders to the Hansens. One of Jim and Gretel's visits came as a result of a common summertime ailment for Southern California dogs – foxtails. Gretel had been favoring her left front paw for a couple of days, so guessing it might be a foxtail, but unable to locate it himself, Jim brought Gretel to my clinic.

Foxtails are like arrows with many barbs, so once they penetrate the skin, they tend to work themselves in deeper, rather than out. As long as it is within approximately one week, the entry wound is usually still visible to the trained eye. A quick examination indeed showed that Gretel had a foxtail in her foot, and it had worked its way up into the area between the toes. Gretel was a very good dog so Briana, my technician, just held her while I probed up into the wound searching for the foxtail. Wounds from foxtails can extend an inch or two up the leg and I suppose it is a bit disconcerting to see a probe disappear quite so far into your own dog's leg. Jim was standing on the other side of the exam table from me, right next to Briana. He watched the entire procedure and seemed very interested in what I was doing, but as I opened the drawer in the table to get out a gauze sponge, I was a bit irritated as Jim leaned way over the table towards me. I was thinking that his curiosity at what was in the drawer was a bit excessive, but then he just laid there. Very quietly and with no fuss, hunky "surfer dude" Jim had passed out cold. After overcoming our surprise and a small bout of the giggles, one of my other technicians, Lucy, came in and helped me lower Jim to the floor and lean him against the wall while Briana continued to hold Gretel.

I was quickly back tending to Gretel. I located and extracted the foxtail, dressed her wound and gave her a treat for being such a good patient. By the time I was finished, Jim was awake and sheepishly took Gretel home. I think we managed to keep that part of the visit from his mom. Sorry Jim, now she knows.

He Recognizes Us

Anita Johanson was an impeccably dressed, soft-spoken, well mannered young woman who owned a beautiful longhaired white and grey Angora rabbit named Emerald. Anita always came across as cool, calm, and collected. Nothing seemed to phase her. We learned differently one day when she brought Emerald in for an ear cleaning. Anita related her wild experiences babysitting for the neighbor's goldfish.

Her neighbors, Joe and Betty Parker were going to be on vacation for two weeks and had asked Anita to fish-sit for them. They had an "only child" named Goldy. Anita agreed, thinking "How much trouble could a little goldfish be?" She was soon to find out.

The day after the Parkers left, Anita accidentally spilled an entire packet of food into the fish bowl. Afraid that Goldy would overeat and die, she successfully scooped out all the excess food. In fact, Goldy probably didn't get enough to eat that particular day. Potential tragedy struck again just a few days later. Anita looked into the bowl one morning and couldn't find Goldy anywhere. She had literally disappeared. Anita's first thought was that Emerald the bunny had somehow gotten into the bowl and eaten poor Goldy. Of course this was preposterous, but the mind doesn't respond well to reason when it's in panic mode. After stewing for a few minutes, Anita decided she would just have to be brave and fess up to the Parkers. She turned back around to look at the fish bowl when low and behold out popped Goldy from the toy castle at the bottom of the tank. Hooray! Another calamity averted. This fish-sitting business wasn't as easy as it was cracked up to be.

Finally, the morning before the Parkers were due home dawned. Anita was so relieved. All of the almost disastrous incidents had worked out. She decided to tidy up a bit and change the water in Goldy's fishbowl. She carefully scooped Goldy and some of her water into a milk glass. "Here we go Goldy, won't it be lovely to have a nice clean bowl?" Anita carefully emptied the rest of the water from the fishbowl, even removing the pink gravel and giving it a good brushing. She scrubbed the bowl, put the clean gravel back in and replaced the little castle that had caused her such a panic earlier in the week. Then she carefully poured Goldy back into her sparkling fresh bowl. "Now, there Goldy. Isn't that much better?" cooed Anita.

Not long after being put in the clean bowl, Goldy breathed her last. Anita forgot that tap water had to be specially treated before it was safe for fish. There are chloramines in tap water that have to be removed before putting fish into the aquarium. There are special products to add to tap water to make it safe, but Anita had not used any. With Goldy's sudden demise, she realized her mistake and immediately treated the water, finding the solution in the supplies left by the Parkers. But Goldy was dead. Did she think it would revive the dead fish? Read on …

In a state of panic, Anita rushed out to the pet store, toting the deceased Goldy in a plastic bag. She found what she thought was an exact look-alike for Goldy and hastily explained her problem to the salesman. He told her how to properly "float" the fish in its transport bag in the new bowl to allow it to adjust to the water temperature. Perhaps all would work out well after all!

But as Anita pulled into her driveway, she couldn't believe her eyes. Coming down the road were the Parkers. They were home a whole day early! This was terrible. How was she going to explain that Goldy was coming back from the pet store? She quickly put the new fish in the bowl without the proper "floating" interval. The doorbell rang just as she emptied the bag into the fishbowl. "So much for floating," she thought. "I hope you're a hardy fish Goldy the Second!"

Betty and Joe hurried over to the fishbowl and peered in, making the same sort of goo-goo ga-ga sounds one usually associates with a baby or maybe a kitten, and there were smiles all around, much to Anita's relief. "Look!" Betty and Joe exclaimed, "He recognizes us!" Luckily, Goldy the Second played along with Anita's ruse. He was resilient and adapted to his new home despite the lack of floating interval and lived happily ever after.

Sheep Tipping

Alice Cranston was one of the biggest animal lovers in Orange Park Acres. This may seem rather inconsequential until you consider that Alice did not have any pets of her own – no horses, no goats, no dog, no cat, no bird, not even a goldfish. Alice was also one of the most loved members of the community, precisely because of her love for animals. She was in her early sixties and had been widowed for several years. She and her husband George had moved to Orange Park Acres about a dozen years earlier as a sort of compromise. It's not that George didn't like animals; he just had not had any experience with them and didn't like dealing with them. He was clearly a "city boy" and didn't like his fine clothes sullied by pet hair. He felt the value of animals was in becoming the meat and dairy products on his dining room table. By moving to the "rural" part of Orange County, Alice was able to enjoy all of the animals in the neighborhood without having any of her own and George did not have to clean cat hair off of his Brooks Brothers suits.

After George passed away, although tempted, Alice did not feel up to taking on her own pets. She did, however, start helping take care of the neighbors' animals, eventually developing into the neighborhood animal sitter. One of her first jobs was to feed Jerry and Jean Kelly's three sheep while the Kellys spent a romantic getaway weekend in San Diego. Very early that Sunday morning, I got a call from panic-stricken Alice. One of the sheep was lying on its back in a drainage ditch with its legs sticking straight up into the air, and she didn't know what to do. Fighting through a woken-from-a-sound-sleep fog, I thought for a moment and then asked her if the sheep was alive. She said yes, it was definitely alive. It was its plaintive cries that had drawn her attention to the problem in the first place, and its legs were waving wildly.

Calling upon the depths of my veterinary training and experience, I then suggested that she go "push it over." Now, she thought for a moment and then said okay, she would try, but requested that I please stay on the phone. Apparently I dozed off, because I awoke to an urgent-sounding, "Lorrie, Lorrie, are you still there Lorrie?" Groggily, I replied, "Yes," to which Alice responded, "I did it." I asked, "So, what happened?" "She got up and walked away. Thank you so very much!" a relieved-sounding Alice exclaimed. We made arrangements for me to stop by later that morning to check on the righted sheep, and I unsuccessfully tried to go back to sleep.

I always liked emergency calls with happy endings, and I especially liked the ones that didn't drag me out into cold, nasty weather. This one had a happy ending and didn't drag me out, but I would have been much happier if she hadn't had to call quite so early to have me help her tip over the sheep.

Zoo Vet

Pre-Senior Moments

As I write these stories, I am old enough to blame all my forgetfulness on "senior moments." Much earlier in my career, however, I can only call them mistakes.

One of these pre-senior moments occurred when I was the emergency on-call veterinarian for the local zoo. Geoffrey, a long-time friend and colleague, was their regular vet. He knew that I aspired to become a zoo vet, so he arranged for me to be his backup. However, in over six months "on the job," I had never been called into action.

I finally got my chance while Geoffrey was on vacation. The zoo curator, Barbara, called Friday afternoon to set up an appointment for me to come to the zoo Monday at 11:00 a.m. to euthanize a sheep. Not exactly "to the rescue" work, but necessary nonetheless. The ewe had tested positive on her TB skin test. Her original owner did not want her back, so the only option was to euthanize her. Barbara had arranged for her to be necropsied at the State Laboratory that same afternoon. It was important to know for sure if the sheep had tuberculosis, as many other animals and several humans had been in contact with her.

I completely forgot about the appointment. At 11:15 a.m. I received a phone call from an irate curator. I apologized profusely, jumped in my car and rushed to the zoo. Twenty minutes later I was greeted by a still somewhat steamed Barbara, and we euthanized the sheep. Fortunately, Barbara made it to the State Lab on time, and better still, learned that the sheep did not have tuberculosis.

Less than six months later, Geoffrey suffered crippling injuries and was unable to continue as the zoo's primary vet. They asked if I would assume the role, and I jumped at the opportunity. Not only did my tardiness not cost me the job, but it also did not cost me a friend. In spite of our rather tense introduction, Barbara and I became close and lasting friends, and I enjoyed many years treating the zoo's animals.

Tying Up Loose Ends

It was a cold (cold for California, that is), windy December day. I arrived at the zoo to be told that Emma, a female emu, had prolapsed. She had about eight inches of tissue protruding from her cloacal opening, but was still contentedly wandering around her pen. In case you're not familiar with bird anatomy, the cloaca is the region of the abdomen the intestinal, urinary and genital canals open into. Essentially, Emma's insides were hanging outside. If prolapsed tissue isn't damaged, it can be cleaned and pushed pack into its proper location. A purse-string suture is then placed around the opening so it can't immediately prolapse again. Each time I pushed from the outside to get the tissue back in where it belonged, Emma would contract her abdominal muscles and push it right back out again. A more intense approach was clearly needed and Emma would have to be put under general anesthesia.

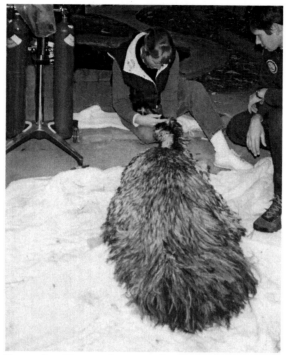

Preparing Emma, the emu, for surgery.

Complication number one: the hospital facility on the grounds was very small and there was really no room in it to work on such a big bird. Solution number one: bring the surgery to Emma. Complication number two: emus, unfortunately, don't have a nice round nose to put into a facemask on an anesthesia machine. Solution number two: we improvised. Ignoring all the warnings on a plastic bag, we put her head into the bag and held it closed tightly around her neck. We then inserted the hose from the anesthetic machine into the plastic bag and delivered the anesthetic gas to her in the bag. Once she was asleep, it was relatively simple to clean and replace the prolapsed tissue. She had prolapsed her uterus, but the tissue looked healthy and I couldn't feel any indication of an immediate problem such as eggs that needed to be laid. Although by no means a common occurrence, such a "for no apparent reason" prolapse is not unheard of. After cleaning and replacing the tissue, I now had to place the purse-string suture in the cloaca, bringing us to complication number three: the emu was lying on the ground in her outside enclosure, where it was cold and windy. Solution number three: I dealt with the cold and lay on the ground beside her to place my suture. As I tried to tie the knot in the suture, I had to have the keeper put her finger on the knot while I finished tying. It felt like we were tying a bow on a Christmas present!

In less than an hour, Emma was up and about as if nothing had happened. She never prolapsed again, but she was never bred, so the full function of her uterus wasn't tested.

He's Having a Baby!

I thought about leaving out the stories that were embarrassing to me, but realized that might shorten the book considerably. It turns out that many of the most entertaining stories are in at least some way embarrassing. The story of Norman is one of the best in this category.

Norman was a male Capuchin monkey, the same breed as Kippy, my first pet monkey. He was one of many Capuchins at the zoo. Not wanting a population explosion, we chose to separate the males and females. We also had all the Howler monkeys we needed, so in late May we created a "bachelor's pad" exhibit with

Norman, two other male Capuchins and two male Howlers. Besides providing an effective means of birth control and avoiding fights over females, we found that visitors enjoyed the mixture of breeds in a single exhibit. Capuchins and Howlers are often found in the same vicinity in Central and South American jungles, so we weren't creating an artificial environment, well, other than having no females.

Just after Halloween, which was about five months after we opened the exhibit, one of Norman's keepers noted that he was bloated and thought maybe he had over-indulged on pumpkins the previous day. All the monkeys love Halloween because lots of pumpkins are donated to the zoo. They love to use the pumpkins as toys. When their new toys break, rather than cry as a child would, they eat them. When I examined Norman, he definitely had a large abdomen but wasn't in any apparent distress, so I elected to leave him alone, instructing the keepers to continue monitoring him.

The bloating increased, so several weeks later, even though he still didn't seem to be in any distress, we caught him and anesthetized him in order to do a more thorough examination. I felt a mass in his abdomen and worried about what kind of tumor it might be. I took an x-ray and when the technician returned with the developed film, she had the biggest smile you've ever seen. She said, "I know what the problem is! Norman – or should I say Norma – is pregnant." The mass in his, I mean her, belly was a fetus. I even had "him" lying on "his" back while waiting for the film to be developed and hadn't paid attention to the reproductive anatomy.

The good news was that Norman's "tumor" was not a problem; the bad news was I've never lived it down.

The gestation period for Capuchins is five to six months, so Norman's husband was certainly one of her current roommates. We made some changes to our bachelor group, evicting Norman in favor of another, carefully chosen male. I don't know who originally "sexed" Norman as a male, but I do know that several veterinarians, me included, had laid hands on him, and no one had ever indicated that Norman was a she.

This Little Piggy Went Home

I was in practice for almost twenty years before I started treating pigs on a regular basis. Mine was a small-animal practice – plus exotics – so horses, cattle and pigs, among others, were referred elsewhere. That was before the advent of the Vietnamese Pot-Bellied pig craze in the mid 1980s. Unlike "real" pigs, which come in many colors and can grow to be 1500 pounds, Pot-Bellied pigs are generally black, or black and white, and weigh 70 to 150 pounds when full grown. Like "real" pigs, they have bristles rather than hair, but their bristles are softer. Hugging a Pot-Bellied pig is similar to hugging a hair brush. They weigh about one pound when they are born and are incredibly cute. They are gentle, very clean, and almost born house-broken. On top of all this, they are exceptionally smart and trainable. They can fetch just like a dog, although maybe not quite as fast.

Monica, one of the founders of the craze, was looking for a veterinarian for her pet pigs. She had visited a few livestock veterinarians who all had experience treating market pigs, but she felt they treated her pigs rather "impersonally." She wanted a vet who would treat her pigs as individuals, as pets, not as members of a large herd. She heard that I treated pet goats, so she showed up at my clinic with some baby pigs! She didn't call to ask – or if she did, she ignored the answer that I did not treat pigs.

She did the wise thing by just showing up with the little black piglets. They were adorable! There was no way I would turn her away. I might actually have paid to get to visit and play with them, but instead I was going to get paid to do just that. And they just needed pre-sale examinations. I explained that I really didn't know much about pigs, but I was willing to look them over for her. She was very knowledgeable about her animals and Pot-Bellied pigs in general. I learned a lot from Monica, did some homework with my textbooks, and happily sent them off with a veterinarian-certified clean bill of health.

Monica came back several times for minor exams and illnesses. It appeared I had met her "treat my pigs as pets" criteria, even though I was totally unaware I was being tested. The work had been quite routine, not really testing my knowledge of pigs until two of her favorite adult pigs, Boaris and Natascha, got into some rat poison. I was now presented with a very tough final exam. I saw those pigs daily for several weeks and both Monica and I did a lot of research on treatment regimens. We even enlisted the aid of my sister, Jane, a medical librarian. Sadly, Boaris didn't make it, but Natascha did and went on to be a good mother, a fine ambassador for the breed, and an over-loved couch potato. It was also the start of a long involvement with

Pot-Bellied pigs for me, culminating in two books[1], and one beloved pet, Piggy Sue.

Arthur van den Bird

Arthur, short for Arthur van den Bird - yet another of Tom's unique pet names – was another crow that shared our house. Like Chirper the mockingbird (on page 115)and LBJ the crow's son (on page 107), he had apparently flunked his first flight lesson and could not get back up into the trees for the night. His parents were nearby and were feeding and attending to him, but Pat Jameson knew that if she left him in the yard, a dog, cat, or coyote would surely eat him during the night. She picked him up and brought him to me.

I raised him in the house (in a cage most of the time) until he was eating well. Then I started taking him outside during the days so he could learn to fly. Once he was flying well, he stayed outside all the time. Always intending to release him, I had handled him very little, but still he formed a bond. Whenever Tom, one of the kids or I walked outside, Arthur would appear, always inquisitive, following us around the yard, watching whatever we did. Even when we no longer offered him food, he was still our nearly constant companion. He had no fear of humans, no fear of our dogs, and he was an unrepentant thief.

---

[1]
Veterinary Care of Pot-Bellied Pet Pigs, by Lorrie Boldrick (1993, All Publishing Company, Orange, CA) and *Pot-Bellied Pigs Mini-Pig Care and Training*, by Kayla Mull and Lorrie Blackburn (1989, All Publishing Company, Orange, CA.

One routine day at work, I was preparing to do surgery on Willie, a large, black and white Alpine buck goat. OK, it was routine for me, not Willie. He had a mass on his abdomen that had been slowly growing for a couple of weeks. It needed to be removed. Because of his size, I set up to do the procedure in a pen in the barn, rather than in the small surgery room inside the hospital. We laid a large green drape on the ground to help keep the surgical field sterile. I unwrapped my surgical pack on the drape and sat on the ground to work. Rob Mason, Willie's owner, wanted to watch the surgery. I had known Rob for many years, so I was confident he wouldn't be a bother, nor would he pass out on me as several of my clients have been known to do. Besides, he was a big guy, and helped us maneuver Willie once he was sedated.

Arthur came to watch, too. He started up on the railing of the pen, getting the bird's eye view, but later fluttered down to the ground. Like a typical crow, he brashly hopped up to the goat (after he was asleep) to see what was going on. Then he spied my open surgical pack and lost interest in Willie. He casually meandered – as well as a crow can casually meander – over beside the pack but kept his eye on Ron. I had noticed Arthur out of the corner of my eye, but my technician and I were focused on Willie and his open belly. Ron told me that as long as he watched Arthur, he would just peck at miscellaneous tidbits on the ground. But as soon as Ron returned his focus to the surgery, Arthur would hop over to the pack intent on stealing an instrument. It became a game of seeing which of them broke eye contact first. Poor Ron missed the entire surgery because he had to watch the crow, but I didn't lose any instruments, and most important to Ron, we successfully removed Willie's tumor.

When I wasn't doing an exciting surgery out in the open, tempting him with shiny, exotic surgical instruments, Arthur went to our neighbor's house to practice his thievery. Jim was building a new deck and Arthur appointed himself helper. Loving shiny objects as he did, he considered all of Jim's screws, nuts, bolts and washers as his prized possessions. The bolts were too large for him to carry, but he did pilfer quite a few of the smaller items. Near the end of the construction project, Jim came by and inquired, "Do you know where Arthur stores his treasures?" He responded to the questioning look on my face by explaining that he was almost done with the deck. He needed just a few more screws and washers and knew that Arthur had stolen at least six or seven. I chuckled, but admitted that I had absolutely no idea where Arthur hid his stash (unlike Poe who I knew had kept his trinkets in the hay and lounge pads). We hunted a little without success, so Jim had to make a trek to the hardware store. We never did find where Arthur hid the goodies he collected. Arthur remained our companion, and a thief, until he succumbed to old age.

Just Kidding ... and Then Some

As a veterinary student, I was taught many things. Some of those things seemed very important and some seemed rather silly. In large animal medicine, we were taught to always check the uterus for another baby if you had helped deliver one. I thought that seemed rather trivial. Of course you'd know if there were more. Little did I realize what a critical role this technique would play in my later dealings with goats.

I had a call one Saturday afternoon from Joe Smith about his Pygmy goat doe, Dasher. In his affected southern accent – he grew up in Southern California, but he was an airplane pilot, and they all seem to speak with a southern accent, Joe included – he calmly told me, "She delivered twins without any problem, but I think there's another kid in there."

Mr. Smith, Dasher, her six kids and five human kids.

"Bring her on over so I can take a look at her," I replied, knowing that multiple births in Pygmy goats were not unusual. He loaded Dasher in the car and made the short three-mile trip to my clinic. Joe slowly got out of his car carrying Dasher and ambled up the drive toward the clinic where I was waiting outside – and yes, he could "amble" while carrying a birthing goat. "Well, since I talked to you, she delivered number three," he matter-of-factly informed me as he reached the clinic entrance, "but please check her anyway. I think there might still be another one in there."

Indeed, he was right. I felt her belly, then reached in and pulled out a healthy baby buck. Remembering that "silly" lesson from school, I told Mr. Smith, "Even though she's already thrown quadruplets, I'm going to reach in again just to make sure there aren't any more." Lo and behold if I didn't feel yet another kid and pulled out a little doe.

"This is amazing," I laughed, "I'd better try one more time." Now it started going way beyond ridiculous, and I was way beyond amazed as I pulled out a sixth healthy kid! This was the first set of sextuplets I had helped deliver. I reached in one last time to try for a seventh, but finally came up empty. Dasher successfully raised all six kids, with a little help from Mr. Smith in the form of supplementary bottle feedings. And you had better believe I always checked for "just one more" after that experience.

Finding (and Removing) the Silver Lining

Have you ever had an eyelash in your eye? Probably you have. I find it very irritating, especially when it seems to take forever to get out. So, imagine how it was for poor Lancelot, a two-year-old Abyssinian cat who effectively had several eyelashes stuck in his eyes for his entire life. Lancelot, possessing the sleek golden look of the breed, was abnormally calm, personable and loving for an

Abyssinian, always enjoying being stroked or held, and he loved to lick faces, especially eyelids. That was somewhat ironic, as his loving personality was not the only thing about him that was abnormal; so were his eyelids.

He didn't have lid margins or eyelashes on the upper lid of either eye. Regular skin grew all the way to the edge of his eye, such that hairs (not technically eyelashes) were constantly irritating his eyeballs. Although by no means a common affliction, neither is it fleetingly rare, and it is routinely overcome by minor surgery. Before I met him, Lancelot had the surgery, but it hadn't worked. Having had success with the procedure on several occasions, I too tried surgery. I cut away lid tissue that was folding under or inward toward the eyeball and placed a couple of stitches to hold the new edge of the eyelid back, but was unable to eliminate the hairs from the edge of the surgical site. He continued to have ulcers on his eyes and was always in some pain. I still don't understand how he could be so happy and loving with that constant pain and irritation. It takes far less to make me grumpy.

It also makes me grumpy to be unable to cure a patient of such a seemingly minor and usually curable problem. Not long after one of Lancelot's follow-up visits, one where I saw that my surgery had failed to rectify the eye pain, I had a revelation – while in the bathroom. While some people say they do their best thinking while in the "library," I had just washed my hands and was gazing into the mirror while drying my hands and scrunching my face in a combination of frustration and perplexity. How could I help Lancelot? That's when it came to me.

I am one of those people who are blessed with thick, dark hair. Unfortunately that includes thick, dark eyebrows, which I don't care for. After many years of being bothered by them, I was lucky enough to find a highly qualified and very nice electrologist. Over the course of five or six short electrolysis sessions, Carley managed to tame my eyebrows quite nicely. In return, a few years later, I found a way to make her job decidedly more interesting.

As I was staring into the mirror, I noticed that my hair and eyebrows weren't all black anymore (a little gray had snuck in). I was reminded of Carley and I got the inspiration that maybe she could help alleviate Lancelot's suffering. I called her that afternoon with my proposal. Understandably, she was a bit hesitant but was willing to give it a try. I checked with Lancelot's owners, and they were all for it. California is among the many states that regulate electrologists, so we figured that taking Lancelot to Carley's clinic was out of the question. Besides, Carley had trouble getting me to sit still while she electrically plucked my eyebrows, so I knew that I would have to anesthetize Lancelot for the procedure. Since there are no regulations about electrolysis on cats, we made an evening appointment for the next week, and Carley brought all her electrolysis equipment to my clinic.

She painstakingly removed all the hairs from the edge of his eyelids. Lancelot's eyes looked better immediately. His owners called me the next day to say the he already appeared much more comfortable. I kicked myself for not thinking of electrolysis before doing the surgery on him. Carley did a second round of electrolysis on Lancelot about six months later, and he has done very well for the last several years. For having been rather hesitant at first, Carley now loves to brag about her four-legged client!

Rabies is Still Dangerous

If you've been reading from the start of the book, you may recall that I had to get a prophylactic rabies shot while in vet school. Sadly, it didn't go well; I passed out as soon as they stuck me with the needle. Fast forward about twenty-five years, and the zoo was adding a colony of fruit bats to their collection. I have always been fascinated by bats, but had never had the opportunity to interact with them. I'm not foolish enough to go places, such as dark caves, where I might accidentally run into one, or vice versa, but I love observing them in zoos. Fruit bats are also know as megabats, but happily, these were tiny megabats. Their bodies were less than three inches long, and their wingspan was about six or seven inches.

For some ridiculous reason, California state law required a rabies vaccination for anyone who was going to handle the bats or be in their exhibit. My desire to be able to treat the bats and my excitement to be close to them overrode logic and my fear of needles, and I agreed to a series of three shots. That's right – three shots, the second coming a month after the first, and the third a month after that. Boy, did I miss the good old days of vet school when the rabies vaccine was only a single injection. Barbara, curator of the zoo and by now a very close friend, accompanied me to the clinic. She, too, was getting the vaccination, but was aware that her primary role was to support me. The nurses were very kind and reassuring when I warned them of my needle phobia, but they were still surprised when I passed out as promised. They were just as kind and reassuring, but much less surprised when I went for the second and third shots, and true to form, passed out again. Some things never change.

Out of the Frying Pan

One weekend afternoon in June, I got a call from Brenda Wilson. She and her husband Ralph, who lived one street over from me, had been out in their ultra-modern eight-stall barn doing chores. They had watched a mule deer weave erratically down their long gravel driveway, try to jump their six-foot chain-link fence, and become hung up in it. Beyond being caught in the fence, it was clearly in distress. Ralph, a graying and balding horse trainer, farrier (a person who shoes horses) and avid hunter had experience with nervous animals. He quickly overcame his surprise at what he had just witnessed, suppressed his hunting instincts, and grabbed the deer. He covered its eyes and carried it into one of their horse stalls. Brenda ran into the house and called me.

While I was driving over, Brenda and Ralph found out part of why the deer was on their driveway. Sue Miller, another community member and avid horsewoman, had been riding her favorite Arabian mare, Sahara, out on the main street in front of the Wilson's home. She saw the deer more staggering than walking down the street. Worried that it would be hit by a car speeding around the corner, she managed to steer the deer down the private drive, assuming it would be much safer. There were just two houses down the private drive so it was essentially a dead-end. Brenda and Ralph, the ones that caught the deer, lived at the very end of that drive.

Just as I drove up, Walt Hopkins, who lived next door to the Wilsons and shared the driveway, was walking up to their house, and more of the doe's harrowing story unfolded. Walt had, coincidentally, been out in his front yard target practicing with his bow and arrow. He said he did a double-take when a deer disrupted his aim by trotting past the hay bale that had his target on it. His surprise was only surpassed by Sue's shock. She was shepherding the deer down the drive, noticed Walt, and then realized what he was doing. She feared that she had herded the deer "out of the frying pan and into the fire!" Luckily, Walt was not a hunter, choosing to shoot at inanimate targets; he would never have shot a deer. He dropped his weapon and followed Sue, her horse, and the deer up the drive. He ended up joining Ralph in the barn stall to help restrain the doe.

The doe was in severe heat prostration and had a few minor injuries from her entanglement in the fence. The guys loaded her into Brenda's Suburban, and we took her to my clinic. I treated her for shock and heat stroke by administering fluids and draping her in wet towels, sutured the larger wounds and flushed the minor ones. As she began to recover and became aware of her surroundings, she started to panic. It was obvious that we had to release her as soon as possible, but we didn't want to let her go where she still might end up in the same predicament. My husband, Tom, called the nearby county park, and the ranger said we could bring her right over, and he would show us a good place to release her. We kept her blindfolded and loaded her back into Brenda's SUV. The ranger led us way back into the park to an area where he saw deer on a regular basis. We got her out of the car and onto the ground and then removed her blindfold. It took her a minute or two

The Mule deer doe happily, and healthily, pronking off into the park after her harrowing afternoon.

to get her bearings before she stood up, took a quick look around and bounded off into the trees. We all cheered for her and were quite proud of ourselves for our afternoon's work.

A Sheep "Pigs Out"

Sometimes an "emergency" is easily recognized – profuse bleeding, loss of consciousness, being trapped by a collar of glass shards (see previous story "Go to the Head of the Line" on page 46), among others. Often, however, it can be hard to define, especially when it involves a loved one, such as a child or pet. Some problems look awful but are really not serious. Other problems don't look bad on the surface, but are truly life endangering. Making the decision of which circumstance you are faced with, and deciding when to call for help can be a challenging dilemma.

Early one weekday morning, Erin, one of Allie's close friends and a fellow member of the local 4-H club, made the decision that she had a genuine emergency. She sounded quite panicked when she called. Erin was a very pretty, dark-haired sixteen-year-old, with a preference for black clothes and dark makeup, what she and Allie described as "Goth." I didn't get it, but she was always quite polite, and happily, Allie didn't mimic her style. Like many teenagers, Erin seemed uncomfortable around adults, so I knew she must consider it an emergency if she was calling me directly rather than going through Allie.

It only took a moment or two before she calmed some and spoke slowly enough that I could understand her. She explained that Natasha, the lamb she was raising to show (and sell) at the Orange County Fair, was choking. Natasha had just begun inhaling her morning scoopful of pellets when she suddenly stopped, backed off from the feed pan and started coughing and gagging. Erin's voice grew higher and faster as she explained that it had been at least ten minutes and Natasha was still coughing and gagging and seemed to be gasping for breath. Realizing that Natasha was not the only one that was becoming quite distressed, I instructed Erin to load the lamb into her truck and bring her to my clinic, less than two miles away. She got her mom to drive, so she could sit in back and comfort Natasha during the trip.

Natasha was indeed choking on her pellets. She had eaten so fast that the dry pellets stuck in her throat and she couldn't swallow them or gag them back up. In a dog or cat, this would be an inconvenience –

uncomfortable but not a major problem. There is inevitably enough air getting to their lungs. If they panic and hyperventilate, they may pass out, but that relieves the stress and either leads to the obstruction resolving itself or allows a calmer trip to the veterinarian. A sheep, however, is a ruminant and must belch excess gas from its stomach frequently. A choking lamb cannot belch, so it is becoming bloated with gas at the same time it is choking. This lamb would die if not relieved in relatively short order.

I quickly passed a stomach tube through the lamb's mouth until it hit the pellets. Pushing on them with the end of the tube proved useless. They wouldn't budge. So I blew on the end of the tube hoping to expand the esophagus around the pellets so they could move on down. Success! The pellets became unstuck. What I had neglected to consider was the amount of gas pressure that had built up in her stomach during the fifteen to twenty minutes the lamb was choking. By releasing the obstruction of pellets, I opened the escape hatch for all that gas and I didn't get the end of the tube out of my mouth quickly enough. Now the lamb felt fine, but I was left spitting out a mouthful, or rather a bellyful, of very foul material. Just the memory of it makes my face and nose scrunch up. Yuck!

Two days later, at about the same time in the morning, Erin called again. She was a bit calmer, but Natasha was choking again. She brought her to the clinic and we repeated the procedure that had been so successful two days earlier. This time, though, I would have received perfect tens in an Olympic event of spitting out tubes. Rather than strive for glory, I chose to cut short my hillbilly Olympic career and devise a method to stop Natasha from repeatedly choking on her food. I had Erin spread out the pellets in a large flat pan full of large, smooth rocks. Thus, the lamb had to pick out the pellets from amongst the stones and could not pig out or wolf them down so quickly. That seemed to do the trick, as thankfully, I didn't have occasion to compete in tube spitting again.

Defend to the (Near) Death

Fred was a lively, four-year-old Jack Russell Terrier. His body was white with the exception of a light brown patch on his back, by his tail. His face was the same light brown, with dark brown rings around his eyes and white around his nose and streaking back up between his eyes to the top of his head. His ears were his most distinctive trait. They looked dark brown, but were actually a mixture of black and tan. His right ear folded forward from near its base, as it should, but his left ear folded about midway up the ear, leaving Fred looking either perpetually-perplexed or ever-inquisitive, depending on your mood or inclination.

Jack Russell Terriers are energetic (i.e., hyperactive) little dogs (typically weighing less than twenty pounds) that are convinced that they are bigger than the largest Great Dane. They were bred in England as working dogs to flush foxes out of their dens, thus their small size coupled with a feisty attitude. Although Fred was a family pet that had never seen a foxhole, let alone an actual fox, he possessed the stereotypical Terrier traits.

George Jones, Fred's buddy and owner, was a novelist who wrote at home, in what he called his "creative room," a converted bedroom covered from floor to ceiling on three walls with bookshelves stuffed full. The fourth wall was mostly glass with French doors framed by large windows that extended almost to the floor. The doors opened onto a brick patio bordered by an expansive yard that backed up to a seasonal creek and walking trail. George oriented his writing desk perpendicular to the windows so he could turn and enjoy the view, but wasn't continuously distracted by it. That was Fred's job.

Fred's bed – a plush, overstuffed leopard-print dog bed with bolsters on three sides – sat next to and behind the desk and next to the window, allowing him to keep an eye on George while also monitoring the backyard for interlopers. If he spotted a squirrel or rabbit in his yard, he would frantically try to scratch through the glass to get at them. George walked Fred several times a day, providing Fred with enough exercise to keep him quiet while he was in the house. They usually went out the back gate and walked along the creek. In spite of his enthusiastic attitude, Fred was well-behaved, so he could run off-leash, splashing in the creek and chasing all manner of critters, some real, some imagined.

On this particular windy and chilly fall afternoon, the creek was dry, but the trail was covered with leaves that were dancing in the wind, keeping Fred busy darting continuously after one, then another, wayward leaf. Fred was so engrossed with the blowing leaves that they hadn't even left the area behind their house when a neighbor and his Rottweiler came down the trail. Neither dog was on a leash. Apparently Fred considered this part of the trail to be his territory or felt threatened in some fashion, because he attacked the Rottweiler, launching himself at its throat. He may have imagined himself as big and strong as a Great Dane, but the Rottweiler almost casually grabbed him with its powerful jaws and tossed him in the air as if he were no more than a piece of brush that had gotten tangled in its fur. Fred yelped painfully as sharp teeth punctured him and thudded ominously as he hit the ground several feet away. His injuries were clearly serious, but he picked himself up and was about to lunge at the Rottweiler again. Luckily, Mr. Jones was quicker than Fred or the Rottweiler and managed to snatch up Fred before round two started.

Mr. Jones wrapped Fred in a blanket and immediately brought him to my clinic. Remarkably, there were no broken bones and only one puncture wound over his chest. After thoroughly irrigating and cleaning the puncture, I put him on antibiotics and sent him home with instructions to flush his wound twice a day. Five days later, Mr. Jones brought Fred back. He was whimpering in pain, unwilling to stand, and smelled like a garbage can. He had gangrene. Although the puncture itself was not very large, when the Rottweiler had bitten Fred, or more specifically, as he threw him away, his tooth had lifted Fred's skin up and destroyed the underlying attachments, which also destroyed the blood supply to most of the skin on Fred's chest. A roughly three-inch by six-inch section of skin was dead and infected. Fred spent a little over a week in the hospital. He had several surgeries to remove the dead tissue and cover the damage with healthy skin grafts taken from his back and hind legs.

Fred was a trooper when we flushed his wounds several times a day, but he really wanted to lick and chew at the wounds. He must have heard the urban legend that a dog's tongue is healing. While a dog's mouth is no dirtier than a human's (depending, of course, on what it most recently ate), their saliva does not have antiseptic or curative powers. Mrs. Jones found a creative solution to the problem. She went to Goodwill and bought infant jumpsuits. Fred was nicely dressed, albeit with hand-me-downs, and his wounds were covered so that he couldn't get at them. The cute outfits were no remedy for the noxious odor the gangrene produced. The nauseating smell permeated the entire clinic, so all my clients that week were aware of Fred and his misadventures. For over a year after Fred was healed and back to normal, clients would come in and ask about that smelly little Jack Russell Terrier.

When a Problem Isn't Really a Problem

One of the biggest challenges of veterinary medicine is that no two patients are alike. Even two animals of the same breed with seemingly identical symptoms may react in drastically different ways to the same drug or treatment. Yet, this challenge is also the source of one of my greatest pleasures in veterinary medicine, in that no two cases are exactly the same. It keeps me on my toes, so to speak, and provides me with the opportunity to learn, which I greatly enjoy. I guess I really enjoyed Pot-Bellied pigs, because I learned many things while treating them, as they were a continual source of ailments and symptoms I had not seen before.

Rosie was a two-year-old Pot-Bellied that Monica had sold to a local retired couple, Don and Jenny Fiorini. They had both grown up on farms in the Midwest, so were immediately attracted to the mini-pigs. Rosie had quickly become part of the family, joining the Fiorinis on their morning and evening walks around their suburban neighborhood, happily trotting along at the end of her neon pink leash, attached to her neon pink halter. Hmm, now that I think about it, her name must have been Pinkie or the leash and collar must have been rose-colored. Don and Jenny got a kick out of the surprised looks they got from passersby, and Rosie adored the attention she got, especially from children. Don would encourage the kids to scratch Rosie on her side, which would lead her to flop over onto her side in pleasure and the kids to scream with equal joy.

I had met Rosie and the Fiorinis on Rosie's routine veterinary checkups. These did not provide any learning experience, but they were still enjoyable, because I got to cuddle and play with Rosie, who was quite a ham. It was soon after she turned two that Rosie provided me with a learning opportunity. Don and Jenny brought her to the clinic because she had suddenly starting losing her hair. It's not as if pigs have a lot of hair to start with, but practically all of it had fallen out in the course of a week. She acted fine and was eating well but she was bald. We did a full diagnostic work-up on her and could find no reason for her hair loss. She showed no other symptoms. Over the next two weeks, while I continued to try to make a definitive diagnosis, Rosie grew back a beautiful coat of hair. I was perplexed because I didn't believe that anything I had done could have led to her cure, but I was pleased she was well.

After the same thing occurred in several more pigs, Monica coined the phrase "chemo-shed." These pigs looked like they had gone through chemotherapy and had lost all their hair. Then it grew back in just fine. I talked to veterinarians all across the country. Since I had

161

co-authored the book *Pot-Bellied Pigs Mini-Pig Care and Training*, many owners gave my name to their veterinarians. Quite a few vets called, clearly as perplexed as I was during my first experience with Rosie, wondering if I had any ideas about pigs that were going bald but acted fine. Eventually I found that some pigs would have a chemo-shed every year or so, and their owners and I learned to just ignore it.

Empathizing with your Pet

Hamlet was a six-week-old Pot-Bellied pig when he came in for his first shots. (As you may have noticed by now, love of miniature pigs must share the same gene with an appreciation of puns, as so many of the pigs I met – including my own Piggy Sue – had quite creative names.) During my examination, Mrs. Riley, Hamlet's human mom, casually mentioned that Hamlet was scratching and rubbing himself constantly. He was a white piglet and his legs had turned an orangish color. Rather sheepishly (as opposed to pig-ishly), Mrs. Riley admitted that she, too, had some funny itchy red spots on her abdomen. This was a fairly easy diagnosis for me; it required a test to confirm, but I was certain that Hamlet and Mrs. Riley both had sarcoptic mange. I had seen it many times in dogs and knew that it could be transmitted by contact to humans. Over time, I learned that Hamlet and Mrs. Riley were not unique. Several other piglets came in with mange. I found one of the easiest ways to diagnose mange in piglets was to ask if the owner was itching too. No new owner could resist cuddling their new piglet up close, so their itchy spots were almost always on their bellies

I treated Hamlet with injections of ivermectin and had him feeling much better in three days and cured in four weeks. I am not, however, licensed to diagnose or treat humans. So Mrs. Riley had to visit her doctor and go through a long explanation of the new pig that slept in bed with her and that the piglet had mange. Mrs. Riley responded well to her M.D.-prescribed treatment and she, too, eventually quit itching. I think that most of my clients got over their personal mange with no treatment, as sarcoptes mites don't really like living on humans, but I would have loved to have been in the doctor's office while Mrs. Riley was explaining her problem.

Another Kind of Multiple

My interest in Pygmy goats started when I treated several for a client and thought they were just the cutest little things I had ever seen. That led me to getting Gabby as a family pet. One turned into many, the Quillie Acres Pygmy herd, which reached a maximum of twenty. I spent three years as the President of the National Pygmy Goat Association and wrote two books on the breed. Going from a complete novice to a twice-published author and President of the national association involves a lot of learning, and a lot of that learning came the hard way – by making mistakes.

I had been breeding Pygmy goats for many years and considered myself very knowledgeable. You can probably sense a mistake coming. I wish I had. Having used Tobin, my own buck, for breeding several years in a row, I decided I needed to introduce a fresh bloodline.

Conveniently, I was able to borrow a handsome, silver-black six-year-old buck from a good friend that lived less than an hour away. I was excited to see the caliber of kids he would produce with my does. I brought Patrick home on a lovely spring day and put him straight into the pen with the four girls. I figured he would breed each doe as she came into season. I never caught Patrick "in the act," but he had sired successfully in the past, and I had never had one of my does go uncovered, so I returned him home after a two-month stay, certain all four does had been impregnated.

Goats have a gestation period of five months. Five months to the day from Patrick's arrival, I noticed one of my does, Mishap, was in labor. "I guess Patrick got off to a quick start," I chuckled to myself. The four mothers-to-be lived together in a big pen most of the time, but I liked to separate them when they were delivering, avoiding any interference and allowing them twenty-four hours to "mother up" with their kids. After that, the whole family, mother and kid(s), would go back in the pen with the rest of the does.

I pulled Mishap out and put her in a private pen and started checking on her frequently so I could watch and/or assist the delivery. On my second hourly visit to check on Mishap, I noticed that Kieran was also in labor. Yikes! I somewhat hastily prepared a second pen and relocated Kieran, too. Only an hour later this time – my next trip down to check on Mishap and Kieran – I went back into the big pen and, you guessed it, found Lisa in labor. Give me a break! Luckily I had a lot of pens. I prepared one more and moved Lisa into it, glad that neither Mishap nor Kieran had actually started dropping kids.

During the short breaks I had between setting up delivery pens, I called Norma, daddy-extraordinaire Patrick's owner, and apprised her of the situation. Being as flabbergasted as I was, I also called a few other goat friends to share my amazing situation. One friend teasingly asked which one I thought would be the first to deliver, and another joked, "Who else is going to go into labor?" I assured her I wasn't pregnant, so it would have to be Sheila! While I almost expected it, I was shocked to find that within another hour, Sheila, my last doe, really was in labor. At least I didn't have to set up a delivery pen, as she was the last one left in the main pen.

So apparently all my girls came into season the moment Patrick came onto the property. He had completed his job on his first day at my house! I could have saved two months worth of goat food. Now that all four does were in labor, the joking took the form of a betting pool to pick which one would deliver first. I picked Kieran – my personal favorite – but I lost. Lisa was first. Sheila and Mishap tied for second, and Kieran delivered almost a full hour later. All four does delivered within six hours!

As I mentioned near the beginning of this story, even as a know-it-all Pygmy goat breeder, I learned something. I decided to change my management techniques if I ever borrowed another buck. He would be introduced to the does individually over the course of at least several days. It was very convenient to have all the kids the same age, but four deliveries in six hours was way more work than I had bargained for, so I would make sure it wouldn't happen again.

Bait and Switch

Mark Rankin lived about a mile from my house. He had raised his two children, Jennifer and Ron, in a sprawling, ranch-style house with a huge yard. It was typical of most of the homes in Orange Park Acres, except he had not used any of his back yard for a horse corral or stable. He was pleased he had decided to stay here after Jeannie, his wife of fifteen years, had died of cancer when the kids were young. He could look around any part of the house and trigger a collection of memories. One of those triggers sat in the center of the back yard – a two-story yellow playhouse with white-shuttered windows and a purple front door. He and Jeannie had built it for Jennifer. The purple door was a compromise, incorporating Jennifer's favorite shade without overwhelming her parents with such a loud color. The door was no longer so shocking, in need of paint, as was the rest of the playhouse. With Jennifer off at college, the playhouse now served as a storage shed.

To combat empty nest syndrome, which struck when Ron headed back east to college two years earlier, Mark bought a beautiful yellow Labrador Retriever named Sunny. She was a bundle of energy and kept Mark well entertained. Sunny considered the back yard her domain, prohibiting entry by any unauthorized visitors, human or animal. She even chased leaves that fluttered down in autumn! At night she was diligent and successful at keeping the opossums up on the fence and out of her yard. During the day, she worked hard trying to keep the squirrels out, but they still managed to sneak in to steal oranges from the trees and food from her very own bag of dog food. The nerve of those pesky creatures! Furthermore, they burrowed under the playhouse and set up housekeeping. They had moved in and planned to stay, causing Sunny endless frustration.

When he discovered the tunnels leading under the playhouse, Mark joined Sunny in her war against the squirrels. I think he was most interested in helping Sunny relieve her frustration, but I'm sure he wanted to save his oranges and the playhouse, too. Mark put poisoned bait inside the playhouse. He knew they were getting inside as well as under the playhouse because he had seen their droppings inside. He knew that Sunny could not get in there, but he put a padlock on the door to be absolutely sure. When he later told me this, I mentally questioned if he really thought she could turn the doorknob, but I appreciated his overly-protective action.

Since she was less than a year old, Sunny had had a chronic sore on the skin on top of her nose. During the summers, the sore would bleed if she licked it excessively. In July of this particular summer, her sore started bleeding more than usual, and Sunny was becoming a bit quieter than normal. It had been a particularly hot summer, so Mark wasn't too worried. He attributed her lethargic attitude to the heat and hoped that some level of maturity might finally be setting in. But, remaining concerned about her bleeding nose, and being a good, cautious parent, he set aside his theories and brought Sunny in to see me. I took a blood sample and sent it to the lab, telling Mark I would call him when the results came back. The next afternoon, Mark and Sunny showed up at the clinic. As I was telling Mark that he need not have stopped by, as the blood work was okay, I squatted down to greet Sunny and saw why they came in person (and dog). The leg I had taken the blood from had swollen to at least twice its normal size. Sunny had bled from the little needle hole in the vein that I had made when collecting the blood sample and the blood had seeped under the skin all around her leg. Her blood wasn't clotting normally, but I couldn't figure out why. She lived in a controlled back yard and there were no poisons in it. I took another blood sample from the other leg for special coagulation tests. Sunny and Mark went home to await the new results, which would take another day.

Mark called fifteen minutes later, proclaiming he had found the problem. The squirrels had carried poisoned bait out of the playhouse and had dropped some of it on the ground outside the playhouse. Sunny was a Labrador and Labradors eat most everything. She had cleaned up all the bait that was available to her, but when they returned this afternoon, Mark noticed her eating something near the playhouse and went to investigate. When he saw the few pellets Sunny hadn't yet consumed, he realized he had poisoned his own dog. At least now we knew what the problem was and how to treat it. Sunny needed a blood transfusion.

Sophie, my own Golden Retriever, graciously donated a bag of blood. She didn't like the process of donating blood, but deep down, I know she was happy to help Sunny out and was proud to have her as a blood sister. I placed a catheter in Sunny's vein and had my technicians hold her very still while we started the blood transfusion. Part way through the procedure, the technician holding her head said, "You have to see this!" I walked up to her head and looked. The continual drip of blood from her nose lesion was now a long clot. The transfusion was working; Sunny's blood was starting to coagulate normally.

While I was doing the blood transfusion, Mark went home to remove the poisoned bait from the playhouse. He decided that the squirrels would have to be evicted some other way. I put Sunny on high doses of Vitamin K and sent her home. Her legs shrunk back to normal size over the next week and she became her normal, happy self again. So much for maturity setting in!

The next summer, Sunny developed a tumor on the tip of her tongue. I referred her to a surgical specialist, and he had to amputate the tip of her tongue. She did beautifully after the surgery and had no problem eating or drinking. The tumor was not malignant, so there was no worry about it recurring. We found an additional, unforeseen benefit of the amputation – she could no longer lick her nose, so she could no longer cause it to bleed. Mark was able to put zinc oxide on it for protection from the sun, and her nose healed very nicely. I'm just glad that the tongue tumor occurred after the poisoning. If her nose lesion hadn't kept dripping blood, we may not have diagnosed her poisoning as quickly and might not have had such a positive outcome.

Learned Her Lesson Well

Isn't it heartwarming to come home and have your dog excitedly wagging his or her tail, so happy to see you? Or to have your cat run down the hall upon hearing your step and sinuously wind around your legs, purring all the while. Clearly, animals learn to recognize their special humans. Sadly, recognizing a human does not always result in tail-wagging happiness, especially when the human is the vet. Many of you have probably experienced your pet's panic upon arriving at a vet clinic. Dogs start to whimper when they get within a couple of blocks of the clinic; cats frenetically try to paw their way out of the car; others save their extreme reactions for the face-to-face encounter with the vet. I have been yowled at, growled at and howled at; yapped at, barked at and bayed at; snarled at, screeched at and bawled at. Luckily, I have been purred at, woofed at, whimpered (happily) at and grinned at far more often.

The variety of behaviors one sees from animals when they recognize a human is not limited to pets and other domesticated animals. Zoo animals also learn to recognize people, including the vet, and greet them in their own inimitable ways.

Ramsey was a Squirrel monkey who clearly thought he recognized me. He always screamed whenever I came near the cage. Apparently Ramsey had an unpleasant experience with a dark haired, medium height woman at some time in his life and he was convinced that mean, terrible person was me. I claim innocence, as I had never treated Ramsey – heck, I had never even handled him for an examination. But that didn't stop him from screaming and jumping about in a rage every time he saw me.

I was therefore quite anxious upon learning that one of the Squirrel monkeys had refused food for several days. There was no way around it; the monkey would need to be examined. I was quite relieved to find out that my patient was Cinder, not Ramsey. Cinder was a gentle monkey, one of several who shared the exhibit with Ramsey. I had treated him successfully in the past, so was confident we would get along fine this time. We did, however, take the precaution of moving Cinder to a separate enclosure for the exam.

I was cautious, but not overly concerned about handling Cinder. Orla, Cinder's keeper, carefully held him immobile while I was doing the examination. Apparently Cinder had listened to one-too-many of Ramsey's stories about me. I made the mistake of sticking my thumb close to his mouth and kind, placid Cinder bit down and wouldn't let go. A second keeper had to pry his mouth off my thumb. Of course, I fainted. In addition, I developed a terrible infection in my thumb that took weeks to resolve. It was so bad, I actually went to a doctor – which is something I don't do very often! Next time I'll consider brushing the monkey's teeth before sticking my thumb in his mouth. Of course that won't stop the fainting, but it may save me from another infection.

Extreme Pet Training

I imagine most of you have had to visit a doctor at some point for an ailment, injury, or routine physical. Even if you're one of the lucky (or stubborn) few that haven't, you're probably familiar with the common need for a urine sample. For men, it's not a big deal, other than possible perform-on-demand anxiety, to aim into the cup. For women, it's a little more of a challenge as we don't have line-of-sight vision, so holding the cup in the right location and catching the sample mid-stream is a bit awkward and sometimes a little messy. OK, a little more information than you really needed, but now let's transition back to the animal kingdom.

Most clients are fine with collecting a fecal sample, as most do that duty while walking their dog or cleaning the cat box. It isn't exactly pleasant, but there is no timing issue involved. Requesting a urine sample from their dog or cat is quite another story. If an owner calls the clinic about a pet that is urinating inappropriately, straining to urinate or that has bloody urine, my technician asks them to bring in a urine sample along with the animal. This request has left many clients speechless, flummoxed and/or dumbfounded, wondering how we expect them to "collect" this sample. Indeed, it can be quite a challenge. Some succeed; some do not.

I had one ingenious young man, George, who showed up with a cup strapped to the end of a fishing pole so when his Jake, his male Rottweiler, lifted his leg on the bushes outside my clinic the sample was safely caught. We got a fresh, mid-stream sample, Jake didn't stop short feeling someone invading his "territory," George's hands remained dry and he didn't have to carry a cup of lovely-smelling pee in his car. A win-win-win-win situation.

Female dogs are harder to collect from since they squat so close to the ground that they even feel a pie tin being pushed under them at the appropriate (or inappropriate, from their point of view) moment. It's amazing how quickly they can turn off a stream of urine. Cats are even harder - they bury their urine. But Jenny never complained about having to collect a sample from Sammy, her seven-year-old Siamese, always arriving with a nice freshly-collected urine sample upon request.

It seems that Sammy would allow her to follow him in to his litter box and hold a pill bottle behind him while he urinated. Sammy had a series of ailments in his seven years, including a few bladder infections, so Jenny had plenty of opportunity to perfect her technique. Just the same, I was amazed when Jenny claimed that Sammy would actually let her know when he was going into the litter box – in case she wanted to come too. I've seen lots of impressive animal tricks, but that one, especially considering its practical use, ranks way up there.

Miracles Really do Happen

Southern California is subject to a myriad of natural disasters. We have floods, landslides, waves crashing into beachfront living rooms, and of course, earthquakes. I've already described a couple of earthquake-related incidents, but fortunately, big shakes occur rarely. Mother Nature (sometimes assisted by man) has one other destructive force she unleashes on us far too often – wildfire. A lot of memories are triggered by the thought of fire, and though no wildfire is a good fire, several of my stories have happy endings.

One such case occurred in the fall after a particularly dry summer. Several large, fast-moving fires erupted in our area. One of those firestorms went through Ortega Canyon where Jane Winchell lived with her elderly grandmother, ten-year-old nephew, two dogs, a pot-bellied pig, and a herd of Nubian goats. Her homestead was near the top of a hill, providing an expansive view of the surrounding countryside. On this particular day, it also provided a clear view of the fire as it ravaged the landscape. When Jane saw that the fire was advancing rapidly toward her house, she prepared to load her animals and move them to a safer area. She had just put Stanley, the pot-bellied pig, into a crate when she realized that the fire had progressed far more quickly than she had anticipated. It had already crested her hill and was literally licking at the back of her house. She opened the crate door, but Stanley refused to come out. She left him, raced to the house, got her grandmother, nephew, and one dog loaded into the car and sped away with the flames tail-gaiting them down the hill. If tears were good firefighters, she could have doused the fire herself as she grieved for all the critters she had been forced to leave behind.

Jane was not allowed to return to her property for over twenty-four hours; twenty-four long, agonizing hours. Having seen how close the fire was to her home, she was not optimistic, but even such a "realistic" attitude could not prepare her for what she faced when she was finally allowed to visit her "home." As she drove up the driveway, it was immediately evident her house was gone. The majestic stone chimney her grandfather had built, normally the first visible part of the home, was not decorating the skyline. When she reached the top of the drive, Jane was distraught with grief and shock. The house was reduced to a pile of still-smoldering ashes. Not even a single two-by-four remained erect. The barn, too, had burned to the ground. What had once been the pig crate, where last she had seen Stanley, was a molten mass of plastic. Total devastation – or so it seemed at first glance.

She was still picturing what less than thirty-six hours earlier had been her home, her ranch, when something broke through her teary-eyed vision. Jane literally shook her head in a sort of double take as she realized that all eighteen goats were huddled in the center of what had been their pen, alive and apparently physically well. The fence that had surrounded the pen was totally gone, but the goats either didn't realize the fence was gone or had seen too much danger outside it to venture away. Then Jane realized what had drawn her attention to the herd. In the midst of the goats stood Stanley the pig, tossing his head up and down and scratching the ground, angrily demanding food and water, just as he normally did at mealtime. The hair on his back was a bit singed – not that pigs have much hair to start with – but he was otherwise unharmed. Miracles really do happen it seems.

Sadly, there was one pet that was not waiting for her – Windy, her seven-year-old Alaskan malamute. Windy had free run of the property, but never strayed too far, preferring to follow Jane as she did her outside chores and lying on the floor wherever Jane was in the house. Jane had last seen Windy when she was racing around the yard, preparing to escape the fire and assumed she had been spooked by the fire and run off. But she wasn't with the goats in their phantom pen, nor did she answer Jane's plaintive cries of "Windy, Windy. Come here girl!" Jane came back daily to feed and water Stanly and the goats – now in their newly-erected corral – to sort through the debris, and to start cleaning up. Each day, with diminishing hope, she called for Windy. A full week after the fire, as Jane drove up the driveway, there she was, lying on the stone porch to the house (sans house). All four feet were so severely burned that Windy couldn't even stand to greet Jane. She tried valiantly but unsuccessfully, and was clearly in pain, but her tail wagged furiously at the sight of her master, causing a flood of tears from Jane. How she had survived for a week and had gotten herself back home was nothing short of miraculous. Jane was overjoyed that Windy had survived, but was terrified by the obvious severity of the burns. Stanley was again forced to wait longer than he preferred for his food, because Jane immediately picked up Windy, gingerly laid her on the passenger's floor of the truck cab and sped to my clinic. Windy's feet were so badly burned that I would normally have suggested putting her down – it would have been cruel to make her suffer the pain of healing those feet – but since she had already survived a week and made such a heroic effort to return home, none of us was willing to deny her the chance to live.

Windy spent a full month at my clinic. She required multiple surgeries and eventually lost the pads off all four paws and the ends of all her toes. For the first week, we had to muzzle her when we changed her bandages twice daily. The second week, she cried while we changed her bandages but did not require a muzzle. By the third week, Windy stoically put up with all of our ministrations. She seemed to sense that we really were tying to help her, not torture her. We carried her outside to enjoy the sunlight each morning and carried her back inside for safety each evening. Jane came by every day to visit and brought In-and-Out burgers for Windy to eat as she categorically refused to touch dog food.

Everyone celebrated when Windy was able to return home on all fours. She still has to wear leather booties to protect her feet when she is outdoors, but she loves to be outside and help look after the baby goats. Windy fought hard to live, and we were all proud to have helped her. Her story ranks at or near the top of the most amazing survival / recoveries I've ever been involved with.

Fluffy Wasn't Fluffy Anymore

Not all fires are "wildfires," but no matter the cause, they can be terribly destructive. Carol and Bill Brown were a retired couple living in a stately, southern-style home in Silverado Canyon. Sitting at the end of a long, tree-lined drive, on the back of a ten-acre parcel of land, the white clapboard, two-story home with its two-story entrance framed by massive columns reminded me of the Tara estate in Gone with the Wind. The resemblance extended beyond appearances to its demise – to fire. Of course, this fire was not a result of the Civil War, but was sparked by some sort of electrical short in the kitchen. The Browns were awakened in the middle of the night by the blaring of the smoke alarm. The fire had ignited in the other end of the house, so by the time they reacted to the alarm, the house was fully engulfed in flames. They didn't have time to collect anything as smoke threatened to overwhelm them.

A passing motorist had spotted the fire and called it in. The fire department responded quickly, saving the major structure of the home, but the damage was severe. The wing housing the kitchen was destroyed by the fire, and most of the rest of the house had water and smoke damage. Happily, Fluffy, their long-haired gray housecat had survived and found refuge in an upstairs closet, but like the rest of the house, she had not gone unscathed.

Word spreads quickly in our community, so I had already heard about the tragic fire the next morning when the Browns showed up with Fluffy. I had never seen Fluffy before, but what I was introduced to – a burned, almost hairless cat that reeked of smoke – made me think the name must be a joke, like calling a big man "Tiny." I hospitalized Fluffy for several days while the Browns looked for a new place to live. Her burns were superficial and not life threatening. Most of her hair must have been singed off by the heat rather than directly by the fire. She also suffered respiratory distress from smoke inhalation, but it too was minor. In spite of her rather ghastly appearance, she could have gone home had the Browns had one to take her to. Fluffy recovered from the trauma quickly, and would rub against the front of her cage and mew for attention when anyone passed her. We were reluctant to provide her the cuddling she desired, though, as she – and the hospital – smelled like a fire zone for the entire time she was there. It was about a year later, after the Browns had returned to "Tara," that they brought Fluffy in for a routine visit and I finally saw why she had been named Fluffy.

Fighting Bucks

Not far from my home and clinic is a large park – popular for picnics, hiking and Frisbee playing. As an added attraction, it has a miniature zoo, which includes an exhibit of deer in a big pen. Years earlier, the zoo had started with just two deer but now had about twenty, and eight of them were bucks. Most of the year they all got along fine, but during breeding season, the bucks fought, battling for the right to breed all the does.

Similar battles go on "in nature," but once a buck is established as the "boss," he often goes unchallenged for several years ... until he is perceived as being old and weak enough to be beaten. In nature, the young bucks (now you know where that term comes from) can head off in search of another herd or at least keep their distance. However, at the park, even with the large pen, the temptation was always very close, leading to seemingly annual scuffles. They resulted in some minor injuries and occasionally alarmed human visitors, but had never required veterinary care until one year, when a young male with a big attitude was killed during a fight. The city officials and I had a conference on how to keep life peaceful in the pen. We decided that we should castrate all the male deer. This would stop the fights and would also control the population which was already too large and growing.

I assembled a special crew for the day. Three of my regular technicians, Briana, Merry and Lucy, came and Lucy brought her husband George along. He was not squeamish about blood and could provide some extra muscle. I also enlisted Barbara, the curator from another local zoo who was an excellent shot with a tranquilizer pistol, to come help. We met two of the park rangers at the crack of dawn. The deer had been fasted overnight (so the tranquilizer would be safer and more effective), but they still had the run of the entire half-acre pen. We set up the "surgical suite" along the side of the barn. I gave the bottle of anesthetic to Barbara and told her the correct dose for the adult bucks. She loaded the tranquilizer gun, quietly crept as close to the herd as she could, and fired. Bull's-eye! While the buck slowly went to sleep (they never go to sleep as fast as they do on TV), I prepared for the surgery. By the time I was ready, the buck was sound asleep. We carried him over to the surgery area, and I prepped him for surgery. I performed the castration first. Then I cut his antlers short since he would no longer have the normal hormonal control to properly shed them. While I was doing the surgery, Barbara shot a tranquilizer dart into the second buck. Once I finished with the first buck, we moved him into the barn where he could slowly and safely wake up. As soon as we got him settled in, the second buck was asleep and ready for my surgical team.

We quickly got it running like an assembly line. As we finished one buck and moved him to the barn, the next was asleep and awaiting. We did all eight bucks that morning, and managed to get most of them done before too many people started arriving at the park. We weren't keen on "shooting" deer in front of the public, even if it was only with a tranquilizer gun. Many would have thought it was cool to watch, but others likely would have focused only on the shooting and considered it cruel.

We kept the bucks in the small barn until they were all wide awake and then released them to join the rest of the herd (the girls). I was super impressed by our great teamwork and was especially pleased that we got all eight bucks done without any disasters. That wasn't the end of the process, though. The park rangers had to stay on their toes for the next six months. Several of the does were already pregnant, so soon after they delivered, we had to catch the fawns and castrate all the little boys. It would have been very frustrating to stop reproduction by all the adults and then let the new babies start the problem all over again.

She's in Charge of the Money

Like a typical movie or television show, this book portrays veterinary medicine as a continuously dynamic job where I'm always on the go, diagnosing an impossible-to-detect condition, performing miraculous surgery or dropping everything to rescue a dying animal. Of course, it's not always like that. I present several embarrassing moments and not-so-happy endings. Yet, even those stories still possess an energy. Among the truly more mundane tasks are bookkeeping and ordering supplies. They don't make exciting copy, but they are a necessary part of the business. Not wanting to leave you with a false impression, let me describe a typical Sunday afternoon going through the inventory printout in my office at home. I determined we needed a case of syringes, marked that on the order form, and was calculating how much gauze we needed when I got a call from the zoo.

A female Great Curassow had been found on the ground by visitors, and her keeper had easily walked up to her and picked her up. A Great Curassow looks like an overgrown chicken with a beautiful curly topknot. A healthy and happy Curassow walks around on the ground but will run or fly away from a visitor or a keeper long before he is within touching range. This bird was neither healthy nor happy. This was very distressing because birds usually don't show clinical signs of illness until they are almost dead. So much for office work (and the description of the boring part of veterinary medicine). Time to drop everything and try to rescue a dying animal!

Barbara brought her to my clinic, but I could find nothing palpably wrong on physical examination. My first thought was "egg-binding." Many female birds will get an egg stuck in their reproductive tract and can become very ill and die unless the egg is somehow passed. I took an x-ray of the Curassow, fully expecting to find an egg. Instead, I saw a pocketful of change in her gizzard (stomach). This bird had heavy-metal poisoning from eating the coins that zoo patrons insisted on throwing into the water in the aviary where the Curassow lived.

Ideally, we would have first treated this bird medically and tried to improve her condition prior to surgical removal of the coins, but she was too far gone to wait. We operated on her immediately and removed eleven pennies, one nickel, two slugs, and one fence staple. Sixteen cents! She tolerated the surgical procedure amazingly well, and we all patted ourselves on the back about saving this bird. I had finished stitching her up, and she was laying in some warm towels. She was starting to move her head around, so I was considering letting Barbara take her back to the zoo. Then, without warning, she took a deep breath and died. It was a perfect example of the old adage "the surgery was a success, but the patient died."

While our attention was focused on the female, we had passing thoughts about her male partner. After commiserating on the loss of the female for a short while, we transferred our concern to the male Curassow, figuring he had also dined on the public's lethal donations. If we could catch him and surgically remove any coins before he got sick, we would all be much happier. He was not showing any signs of ill health, so it wasn't simply a matter of walking up to him and carrying him to the x-ray machine. The keepers set a trap they had for just such occasions, and in just a couple of days they caught him. We took an x-ray, and happily there were no coins at all in his gizzard. We were quite relieved, surmising that his wife handled all the money in their family. The true moral of this story is, "Please don't throw coins in the water in animal exhibits even if there are no signs prohibiting it! You may think it is supposed to bring you good luck, but it brought only bad luck to the Great Curassow."

Counting Sponges

Louise Cornelius was one of those people who couldn't say no to an animal. She rescued them all, but she primarily rescued cats. She found lots of homes for lots of cats, but if she couldn't find a suitable home, she kept that particular rescue. As a result, she had lots of cats – and named and loved them all. At one point, I think she had fifteen cats living with her! They were all extremely well cared for, but I swear Louise must have had to spend a couple hours a day cleaning cat boxes.

One of the first rescues she personally adopted was a long-haired white cat that she named Blackie. Louise did have a sense of humor. Blackie was a female that had been spayed sometime before Louise found her. After seven years of cat-bliss living with Louise, Blackie started looking a little bloated, but was not eating well, so it wasn't natural weight gain. Louise tried spoiling her with high-end cat food and even some fresh fish, but Blackie still was not up to snuff, so Louise brought her in for me to examine.

As I palpated Blackie's abdomen, I felt a large mass, but couldn't really decide what it might be. It wasn't as I had hoped, a superficial lipoma (fatty tumor). The mass was fairly large and firmly attached to the abdominal wall, and I couldn't escape thoughts of cancer, but it didn't quite feel like any other type of tumor I had experienced. Louise was already harboring similar fears, so my diagnosis was not very comforting. Even with a herd of cats to support, she was ready to spend whatever was necessary if I thought it might benefit Blackie. If such a large mass was indeed cancer, I was skeptical that its removal would significantly improve Blackie's condition, but I was curious as to its not-normal feel, leaving a shred of optimism. We scheduled an exploratory surgery, prepared to excise the large mass, or if it wasn't operable, to not let Blackie wake up from the surgery.

Louise brought her beloved pet back in for surgery the next day. As I was making my incision, I immediately started to worry. The mass was firmly attached to the abdominal wall right next to my incision – not a good sign. I decided to try to peel it off and find its primary source. I was not happy with how the surgery was progressing. Non-malignant tumors are usually quite discreet, but this mass was diffuse and definitely not discreet. As I was peeling it off the abdominal wall with my hands and small cuts with a scalpel, it suddenly ripped open … and I found a gauze sponge! It had apparently been left in when Blackie was spayed over seven years earlier. I don't know how she stayed so healthy for so long, and I don't really know why the sponge was suddenly bothering her. Who cares?! It wasn't cancer. With a great sigh of relief, I removed the sponge and all the fibrous tissue around it and knew that Blackie would be fine. Blackie, Louise and I were all very happy with the outcome, and we were all glad that we had given her a chance with the surgery. And since then, I've been even more diligent about checking my surgical field for stray sponges before closing every incision!

The Moral of the Story

A fable is a short story that teaches a lesson and has a moral. It is usually fictional and the characters are often animals. All the stories in this book involve animals, but even though many have been embellished, they are all based on fact. That doesn't stop some of them from having rather poignant morals. I learn from every case on which I work; some of the toughest lessons coming when I've made a mistake. Learning from the mistakes of others can save you a lot of pain. Here's one such opportunity that I certainly took to heart.

Rover was a well-behaved, one-year-old Labrador Retriever. His owner, Sam, a twenty-five-year-old construction worker, took Rover everywhere, even to work at the construction site, where he would lounge in the shade of the truck and entertain the guys during breaks, chasing after tennis balls or scraps of two-by-four. Every afternoon after work, Sam and Rover went for a walk at the dog beach, a local park or just around the neighborhood. They were best buddies. One day as they were waiting at the corner of a busy street during their walk, a car backfired and spooked Rover. He instinctively recoiled from the sound, which allowed him to slide out of his ordinary buckle-type collar. Without a leash to restrain him in his panic, he raced away from the noise into the adjacent street. He was hit by a car and killed instantly. Sam was devastated.

Sam has a new Labrador now and they too go for daily walks. But now the dog wears a choke collar with the leash properly attached at all times. If another car should backfire, the dog may back up, but he will not slip out of his choke collar. I certainly have learned from Sam's misfortune, and my dogs now always wear a choke collar whenever we leave our property. So does my brother Mikey's Labrador, Bashan. She's amazingly well-trained and obedient, but Mikey can empathize with the tragic loss of a deeply-loved companion and understands that some brief discomfort for Bashan if she were to spook is far better than knowing he failed in his responsibility to watch out for her. Besides, he knows I would disown him (or worse) if I learned she was injured or, heaven forbid, killed because she slipped her collar.

Some owners tout the use of harnesses, claiming they are more "humane" than regular collars and especially more so than choke chains. I disagree – strongly. Using a harness trains a dog to pull. Harnesses are for sled dogs, so they can pull efficiently without any pain or discomfort. Sled dogs are painstakingly trained to respond to the commands of the musher, pulling and stopping on command. Using a harness for routine walks does not provide any negative reinforcement for pulling. Rather it seems to teach the dog to take its owner for a walk, rather than the reverse. While it may be kind of fun for the dog, it doesn't look very enjoyable for the person being dragged behind.

Choke collars only hurt when the dog pulls at the end of the leash. When the dog stops pulling, the choking stops. Just as it should be. Proper use of a choke chain – a short, sharp tug when the dog starts pulling on its leash – is an effective means of training the dog to heel, to remain under your control while you are walking. The dog will learn quickly and you'll rarely have to pull on the chain, and you both will avoid the pain Rover and Sam suffered.

Are You my Mother?

You don't need to be a veterinarian for people to choose you as the appropriate caretaker for young or injured critters. Sometimes even having worked as a veterinary assistant makes you a target. Mikey had the additional credential of having me, a veterinarian, as a sister. He and Quin were living in semi-rural Lake Elizabeth, a community about an hour north of Los Angeles. One day, their neighbor Christine appeared at the front door with a bucket. Inside was a very young baby ground squirrel that her Bull Mastiffs Vicki and Sammy had discovered in her barn yard.

Christine noticed the harmless but mischievous pair focused on something in the corner of the yard, and experience warned her that it would be wise to investigate. The little squirrel undoubtedly agreed. The dogs were both down on their forepaws, butts up in the air, tails wagging excitedly. They seemed fascinated by the little guy, sniffing him and nudging him with their noses, trying to coax their new toy to move. The poor thing didn't seem too interested in playing – more like he was panic stricken. Christine figured he was too young to be separated from its mother, so rather than simply release him in the open field just outside her fence, she brought him to her next-door neighbor Mikey, the former veterinary assistant. Surely he'd know what to do, and he did – he called me and asked what he should do.

My original care advice probably violated all aspects of the Hippocratic Oath and probably the Geneva Convention. Confused? Let me explain. I love animals, and we'd had a wonderful pet squirrel, Princess Leia, but ground squirrels (as opposed to tree squirrels) can be very destructive. My bias against them grew largely out of their attempt to undermine my business, and I mean literally undermine it. They tunneled extensively under my barn, causing some minor structural damage. I trapped dozens of the scoundrels and released them in a local park. It was a very frustrating battle against a seemingly endless supply of squirrels. The more I caught and relocated, the more that that seemed to appear under my clinic. I finally enlisted teenaged Quin to "eliminate" the pests using his trusty and beloved pellet gun. The bounty was five dollars each, and he made a good living for a few months.

It was now several years later, and Mikey was unimpressed with my suggestion that he enlist Quin to "care" for the squirrel. I relented and gave him proper care instructions. He traveled thirty miles to the nearest drug store to get an eyedropper and to a pet store for formula. My instructions included minimizing his contact with the baby so it wouldn't become too comfortable with humans, but more importantly, not to let Dagny, his twelve-year-old Golden Retriever, befriend the little critter. Thinking dogs are friendly could prove deadly to a wild ground squirrel. I recommended a wire cage, so once "Squirt" was weaned, Mikey could put "Squirt" out in the field, next to a nest, to reintroduce him to his own kind. Unfortunately, I did not specify the spacing between the wires.

One evening, Mikey walked into the kitchen to check on Squirt, only to find the cage empty, but the door closed. As Quin was not home, he could not accuse him of making the squirrel disappear, so in a mild panic, he started scouring the house in search of the baby squirrel. Dagny seemed unconcerned by his panic, remaining curled up on her blanket When he was about to give up, Mikey stopped to give Dagny a pat, only to discover why she had not joined him in his search. She knew exactly where Squirt was ... curled up against her belly. It had been almost ten years since she had had a litter of thirteen puppies, but she seemed to retain the protective maternal instinct.

Princess Leia appreciated Quin's dislike of bread crust. Hmmm. That looks like a lot more than just the crust, Quin.

Mikey made another trip down to the pet store to buy a cage with much smaller spacing between the wires. After another week of escape-free bottle feeding, it was time to release Squirt. Mikey set the cage next to a rock pile in the empty lot behind his house. He could see it from inside the house and knew that it served as home to squirrels. The first two days he left the cage door shut and brought it in at night. On the third day, he opened the cage door, but Squirt was still there at the end of the day. On the evening of the fourth day, Mikey found the cage empty, but familiar chirping from under the overhang of a rock alerted him that Squirt was still nearby. Mikey left the cage with the door open and with fresh food and water. The food and water went untouched for the next several days, so it seemed Squirt had been accepted back into the wild squirrel community, although we don't know if he tried to befriend any more dogs.

Blow for Me, Please

As you have undoubtedly noticed by now, throughout my career I've worked with an amazing array of animals, from aardvarks to zebras. Well, not aardvarks or zebras, but I have treated wallabies, llamas, lemurs, bats and scores of other wonderful creatures. Perhaps the most thrilled I've been to get a new client was when I was contracted to look after the dolphins at a local amusement park. Dolphins are considered one of the most intelligent mammals, and their size, strength and playfulness are amazing.

One of my first dolphin patients was Rosie. The six-year-old female had been coughing for several days, and her trainers were concerned. She was still performing normally during shows and eating well, but she had a persistent cough with more severe coughing "fits" several times a day. Shirley, Rosie's trainer for most of her life, had her perform for me so as to induce her cough. It didn't take much to get Rosie to cough, and I quickly agreed that it was causing her some distress. Listening to her heart and lungs through all that blubber – not that I'm calling you fat, Rosie – is tough, especially on the pool deck, but I heard congestion in her lungs, so I suspected some sort of infection. I really needed to identify the cause of the infection, so I had to take a culture of her blow hole.

A dolphin's intelligence includes a good memory, and all the dolphins at the park were quick to identify me as a veterinarian, or as they would probably have put it, "that mean lady that pricks and prods us and does all sorts of other rude things to us." Given that, no way was Rosie going to let me do the culture procedure. She was infinitely more trusting of Shirley, allowing her to do most anything to her. Shirley and Rosie had been working on blowhole cultures since before I was the vet – it wasn't just me, but any veterinarian that the dolphins weren't fond of. Shirley would instruct Rosie to "blow" and then stick the sterile end of the culture swab into the open blowhole. Rosie would close her blow hole immediately and hold still until told to blow again. Then Shirley would pull out the culture swab and we could package it appropriately and send it to the lab.

We usually used culture swabs with wooden sticks and I always worried that the stick would break off in the dolphin's blowhole while the trainer was holding it, waiting for the next breath. So I thought I was being very smart to bring culture swabs that had fine metal stems instead of wooden stems. Rosie would be the first trial. She came to the side of the pool and opened her blow hole on Shirley's command. Shirley inserted the metal swab. Rosie clamped her blowhole shut and took off like she had been stung, the swab still in her blowhole. She swam far out in the pool and stayed down deep enough that we couldn't see her. She stayed out there for what seemed to be a very long time. Shirley and I were both beginning to panic – at least I know I was. Did Rosie inhale the swab? Was she in respiratory distress … and underwater? I pictured a thousand terrible things that could be happening. Eventually she surfaced and we both breathed a huge sigh of relief. She came back up to the side of the pool in front of us, and there between her teeth was the swab, which she carefully "handed" to Shirley. She had apparently blown the swab out of her blow hole and then stayed underwater while she tried to pick it up so she could bring it back to us. It was almost a moment for tears, I was so happy to see her – and the swab. In retrospect, I imagine that the salt water and the metal stick caused some sort of electrical reaction like the static shock you get when you touch metal during dry weather. It was enough to scare her into swimming away and eliminating the stick from her blowhole. My metal swab trial ended abruptly at one!

Lest I leave you wondering how Rosie fared with her cough, the culture – obtained using a wooden swab – identified a bacterial infection that we treated with a targeted antibiotic. Rosie was back to her cough-less self in less than two weeks.

Cough It Up, Louie

Another dolphin, Louie, developed respiratory symptoms in the form of a persistent cough. His symptoms more severe than Rosie's, so a simple blowhole culture (remember how "simple" Rosie's was?) wasn't going to do the trick. I wanted to examine and culture cells from deeper down in his lungs. No problem! I'd just ask Louie to cough real hard for me, and I would be set. Surprisingly, it wasn't much more difficult than that, at least for me.

Guess what Louis is going to do with the ball. ... Throw it, of course! What did you think I was going to say, "cough it up?"

Most everything I did with the dolphins required their full cooperation, and most often it also required them to be taught a special behavior. In just a couple of days

Shirley taught Louie to "cough," meaning blow very hard through his blow hole. I was, and still am, very impressed at Shirley's ability to train dolphins to perform on command. Not to lessen the respect she deserves, this particular "trick" probably wasn't so hard to teach, since Louie was coughing incessantly. Shirley just had to get him to do it on command and to step it up a level (i.e., blow hard). Blowing hard would expel the material that I needed from deeper in his respiratory tract.

When it was time for Louie to perform for his audience of one – me – I held a culture plate several inches above his blow hole and Shirley told him to cough. He should have earned double reward, because he blew so hard that the culture plate flew right out of my hand and into the water. Shirley and I both laughed at my lack of holding skills, and I think Louie even laughed at me. At least it sure looked like a grin on his face as he retrieved my salt water culture. I got a new culture plate so we could repeat the process. This time I held on much tighter and did succeed in getting my sample. The laboratory identified a rather nasty infection that was going to require more than oral antibiotics. I was going to have to shoot Louie … in the tail … with a syringe … to get a blood sample and later to deliver the appropriate drugs. Fortunately, presenting its tail and accepting the momentary pain of being stuck with a needle is part of a dolphin's basic training. Louie took it like a man – actually with less crying than most men – and responded well to the antibiotics.

Not Even if You Ask Nicely

Coughing is a natural behavior, so teaching a dolphin to do it on command is not exceptionally difficult. You catch him or her coughing naturally and immediately deliver the word, or in this case hand signal, you want to associate with the behavior, along with a reward, and the dolphin catches on very quickly. Training works quite similarly with dogs and humans. Well, men are sometimes kind of slow to catch on.

Anyway, Shirley knew that training a dolphin to present its tail, while unnatural, was important to ensure that blood could be drawn or shots administered when necessary. It's one of those "it's for your own good" kinds of things. So, she trained all the dolphins to present their tail on command. Shirley would sit on the side of the pool and the dolphin would turn so whoever was with her could reach the tail flukes and pull them up into his or her lap. Theoretically, if I was the one sitting next to her, I could then feel along the fluke, find the vein and get my blood sample. Theoretically. In practice, it didn't quite work that way.

As I've mentioned previously, dolphins are smart, and they have good memories, especially when it comes to the veterinarian. In anticipation of my visit to obtain a blood sample from Louie, Shirley and several different volunteers spent a couple of days working with him. Shirley would command Louie to present his tail, and Louie would, without fail, politely obey. The volunteer would pull his tail up into his or her lap and poke on the tail as if preparing to draw a blood sample. No problem … until it was me instead of a volunteer. Apparently the fake vets must "poke" at the tail differently than I do, because as soon as I touched his tail, Louie took off.

Bad Louie! Shirley gave him a "time out," meaning we ignored him for a couple of minutes and then asked for the behavior again. He politely presented his tail to me, but as soon as I touched it, off he went again. Bad bad Louie! This was to be my first blood draw from a dolphin, and I was quickly becoming discouraged.

After another "time out" we tried again, and "hooray!" this time he not only let me pull his tail up into my lap, he also let me draw blood. Good Louie! As it turned out, Louie was not alone in his reluctance to let me handle his tail. Every other dolphin made it a habit to swim off the first time I touched its tail, but almost always submitted the second time. Maybe they were just trying to prove that they knew the difference between a training session and the real thing.

Dead But Not Forgotten

My best bite-wound story is being bitten by a dead iguana. Yes, a dead iguana! You don't have to read any farther to agree that this must be an interesting story. Being bitten by an iguana is pretty unique; being bitten by a dead iguana seems downright impossible. Alas, it is not, and I have the scars (physical and emotional) to prove it. So, how did I manage to accomplish this inconceivable feat?

Fernando, a twenty-four-inch-long iguana, belonged to a local zoo. He was part of their education collection, being docile enough to be handled by school children. He grew to be far from docile, however, actually acting rather aggressive with the other iguanas in his exhibit at the zoo. It may have been the other iguanas picking on Fernando because of jealousy over his star status, but it sure didn't look that way. Regardless, he was involved in all the disputes, causing minor injuries to other iguanas and himself, so we decided that castrating Fernando might quiet him.

The zoo had a small (considering some of the animals we had to treat) but reasonably-well-equipped veterinary clinic, so we performed Fernando's surgery on-site. This way, the keepers could easily monitor him and provide post-surgical care. Castrating an iguana is not nearly as simple as castrating a dog or a goat. While a male iguana's testes are larger relative to its body than those of other animals, iguanas themselves are smaller than most animals I treat. More significant in this case, the testes are in the abdomen as opposed to in an external scrotum. Since the surgery involved an abdominal incision, we had to use general anesthesia, a challenge with such a small and exotic creature.

In spite of how difficult I just made the procedure seem, the surgery went smoothly and I finished neutering Fernando in about forty-five minutes. I was washing my hands when Barbara called out, "Come quick, I think Fernando just died!" Indeed, he was limp and not breathing. I opened his mouth (no, not to give mouth-to-mouth) and got no resistance. I grabbed an endotracheal (breathing) tube and while using one finger to hold his mouth open, started to pass the tube down his throat, much as I had done at the start of the surgical procedure. The difference this time was that we were no longer administering anesthesia (especially since we thought he was dead). Well, Fernando came back to life – with a vengeance – and chomped down on my finger. It took two people to pry him off, and I subsequently passed out. What a surprise! Having supported me through several fainting incidents, Barbara anticipated my collapse and was holding me with one arm while helping to extract Fernando from my finger. Other than a couple of punctures and a very sore finger, I was fine, and in spite of his rather unappreciative behavior, I'm happy to report that Fernando is alive and doing well and probably still bragging about how he fooled me.

Holding Up Your End

In my many years practicing veterinary medicine, anesthesia has always been one of my biggest concerns. There is a risk giving any drug to an animal, or human for that matter, but anesthetizing an animal has always seemed to me to be one of the most important responsibilities of my profession. So, whenever I can safely perform a surgery with local anesthesia, I usually do.

One such case was with a member of Steve Kennedy's reptile collection, one of his red-tailed boa constrictors. Bertha was a big girl, about ten feet long, and had a small mass on the side of her neck, just an inch or two behind her head. We had watched the mass for a month and it had not subsided, so we decided it was time to remove it. I wanted to use a local anesthetic so I needed several people to hold her for the procedure. Since I did the surgery at Steve's place, his employees helped me. Carla sat in a chair and held the head steady on the operating table for me while the front of the body draped down and rested in her lap. There wasn't room for more chairs, so Andy and Louise stood to the side of Carla and held the middle and the tail end of the snake, respectively. Steve was on the opposite side of the table, near me, observing. He had offered to help, but when I don't know a client well and have sufficient staff, I prefer to use just my staff. For most general surgeries, I prefer the client not even be in the room, but this was a clean, simple procedure.

Bertha was a very nice snake, but no snake likes to be restrained tightly. I injected the local anesthetic around the mass and we waited for five minutes for the drug to work. I cut over the mass and removed a core of yellow, granulomatous material (better known as pus). I cauterized the lining of the wound and stapled it shut. Just as I put in the last staple, I heard Steve ask, "Louise, what are you doing? Are you OK?" She had just collapsed to the floor. As it turned out, it wasn't queasiness that sent her to the ground, but a combination of a bad cold and too much cold medicine. Either way, I was so happy she had waited until I was finished with the procedure before she quit holding her end of the snake.

International Vet

Modern Conveniences

My practice expanded outside Southern California when Barbara and I planned a trip to Costa Rica. She had a friend, Katherine, who was president of a non-profit organization that owned and operated a biological research station in Tortuguero. Cano Palma Biological Research Station was not a four-star hotel. It housed researchers when they were working on local projects. At other times, the bunk house was rented to visitors. We signed up to be two of those visitors.

Shortly before we were to leave, Katherine called Barbara and asked if I would be willing to spay two cats while we were there. She had allowed the station manager to adopt two cats, but was having second thoughts about keeping two small predators at a station designed to view and study wildlife – particularly birds. If she was going to allow them to stay, she wanted to be sure they would not reproduce. They were both girl cats, and we all know that birth is already controlled with only two girls, but Katherine felt obliged to guarantee that her girls were safe – just in case a tom cat happened by. So I took a surgical pack and some anesthesia in my luggage with no knowledge of what I was getting myself into.

Tortuguero is a very small village on the northeast (Atlantic) coast of Costa Rica. It is not accessible by road, only by boat or plane. The airport consists of a paved landing strip located about a mile from the village. There's no Airport Sheraton, no restaurant, no

Starbucks, not even a terminal building. The planes land, unload passengers and luggage beside the runway, and then take off again. If no one is there to pick you up in a boat, it's a tough hike through the jungle (rain forest) or a long swim through Cayman-infested (alligator-like creatures) water to any human habitation. The research station is a half-hour boat ride farther down the canal from Tortuguero, in the rain forest, in the middle of nowhere.

We had left Los Angeles Tuesday evening, flown through Miami and on to San Jose, the capital of Costa Rica, arriving early Wednesday morning. We spent the day walking around San Jose, as we were booked on an afternoon flight to Tortuguero. Being a rain forest, rain and thunderstorms are common in the Tortuguero region. Our tiny commuter flight ran smack into a storm, bouncing us, along with several local residents returning from business in San Jose, most of the way. Barbara suffers from motion sickness, and the bumpy ride in a small plane left her feeling nauseated and exhausted. We were anxious to get to Cano Palma, get settled in, and get some sleep. Alas, our transportation for the final leg of the journey wasn't at the airport to meet us! We huddled under a tree, avoiding some of the rain and waiting hopelessly for somebody to show up to pick us up. The plane left on its return trip, and all the locals headed off leaving us standing there helplessly. A local fisherman took pity on us and gave us a ride into Tortuguero, where he introduced us to another fisherman who was willing, for a fee, to take us on down the canal to Cano Palma.

As it turns out, the small planes "never" fly in the conditions ours did, so our host at the research station had assumed we wouldn't arrive until the next morning, thus he had not come to pick us up. By the time we arrived at Cano Palma, the weather had cleared and jungle-filtered, late-afternoon sunlight shone on the camp. Other than hurricane lamps, which had yet to be turned on, this was the only light, as there was no electricity at Cano Palma. Nor was there any indoor plumbing.

Water came from a "well," which was actually a covered hole in the ground. A cast iron pot with a long rope attached to it sat on the cover. To get some water, you had to drop the pot in the hole and pull it back up with water in it. We had drunk all the bottled water we had brought with us during our adventurous trip to the station, and we were very thirsty, so I went to fetch some. It looked easy enough to me, but when I dropped the pot down, it landed bottom first and just floated on the surface. Several attempts to submerge the pot by jiggling the rope failed to get it to fill with water. It was quite a challenge to drop the pot at the proper sideways angle to have it actually submerge. Plus, I had to keep holding on to the rope, too!

Eventually I succeeded in bringing a pan full of water up out of the well, but our thirst was still not quenched, as it was not potable water. We put some of the well water on the propane stove to boil, but we didn't want to wait for a drink. Anticipating issues with water, we had purchased iodine tablets for water purification back in the States. We put the right number of tablets in some water and carefully followed the mixing instructions. The resultant water may have been safe to drink, but it tasted so foul that we both elected to wait until the water on the stove boiled and then cooled.

Cano Palma was a lush, tropical camp. The bunkhouse had four rooms with two cots in each room and a screen covering the windows. The rooms weren't large, but were more spacious than I had expected, having a bedside table between the cots, and a small desk and dresser at the foot of each. Since the normal guests were researchers who might stay for several months, they had provided a modicum of comfort and personal space. The bunkhouse, like all the buildings, was on a raised post foundation because during the rainy season, the entire camp would flood. The kitchen, which consisted of a propane stove and a table, had a roof, but no walls – sort of an alfresco experience. It was to serve as my surgical suite, with the dinner table, a picnic bench with a vinyl tablecloth, acting as the operating table.

Barbara prepared for the surgery by washing the tablecloth as well as possible. I anesthetized the first cat and brought her to the surgical suite. A cat needs to lie on her back during a spay surgery. In my clinic in Orange, I have a plastic "V" form to help keep her balanced and we use leg ties to keep her legs stretched out of the way of the surgery area. At Cano Palma, Barbara improvised by tying the cat's hind legs to a stick to keep her positioned correctly. I used scissors and a disposable razor to shave her belly. I may do better at home with a pair of electric clippers, but I was impressed with the quality of my low-tech prep job. Barbara scrubbed the cat's shaved belly while I scrubbed my hands. We even used the boiled water – just like in old time movies. One of Barbara's jobs for the duration of the surgery was to keep flies and other flying insects out of my surgical field. The surgery was successful and we proceeded to do the second cat the same way. With all this primitiveness, I was happy it wasn't raining, although even at eight in the morning, it was very warm and humid. Then again, it was a rain forest. The two cats were restricted to an out-building for the week post-surgery, minimizing their physical activity and ensuring their incisions would remain clean. They recovered well and were released from the building the day we left the camp.

Preparing for surgery al fresco - in the Costa Rican jungle.

That experience certainly made me appreciate the modern conveniences I take for granted at home. Doing without electric clippers, a good surgical light and a height-adjustable table was an inconvenience. Doing without my electronic monitors during surgery was more disconcerting. Barbara had a stethoscope and monitored the cat's heart and respiration regularly – when she wasn't swatting flies. What I missed most was the continual "beeping" of a monitor telling me that the animal's heart was beating.

Offshore Medical School

Barbara and I visited Cano Palma four different times. Progress was made at the station between each of our visits. By our last visit, the kitchen was fully enclosed, there was electricity (most of the time), and they had acquired a male dog (I consider that progress).

Pedro was an eight-month-old Labrador Retriever mix. He was a big brown dog weighing about sixty pounds. There were no other dogs in the area, but Katherine was still president of the Cano Palma non-profit organization and she felt the station must demonstrate responsibility and castrate their dog. Since I was planning a visit, I was recruited to again control the domesticated wildlife population (perform the surgery).

My daughter, Allie, was a sophomore in medical school at the time. As our trip coincided with her spring vacation, she decided to come with us to visit this unique part of Costa Rica that few tourists get to see. Two of her classmates also chose Cano Palma in lieu of Florida, Cancun or other more traditional spring break venues. Katherine said there was room for all five of us, and we would have a bunkmate. Sonya, a petite, dark-haired biology graduate student from a French-speaking area of Canada, had been there for two months and still had one more month before she went home. She was working with the station manager on an avian research project, helping with general station maintenance and learning a lot about local ecology.

I figured that the Pedro's surgery would be a great educational experience for all four girls. They could all watch and maybe even assist with a true "field surgery." The kitchen would again be my surgical suite, however, with all the "modern improvements," there would be no need for a continual fly swatter. Where were all these assistants when I needed them on our first visit? There was still no air conditioning, but it was early spring, and happily, the weather was relatively cool. Surgery was scheduled for the first morning of our visit, but the station manager forgot and fed Pedro breakfast, so we postponed surgery for a day. Our journey from the States to the research station had been much smoother than the first time, but we still took advantage of the opportunity to sleep in a little, relax and explore the area.

Early the next morning, I anesthetized Pedro. Even though I knew they had electricity, I opted to not pack my electric clippers and instead shaved his groin with a disposable razor – and I did an excellent job if I do say so myself. Pedro's surgery went very smoothly, but my students/assistants/audience did not fare so well. Georgia, one of Allie's classmates, had decided to sleep in and didn't watch the surgery at all. Just after I made my incision into the scrotum, Sonya had to leave before she fainted. Melissa, Allie's other classmate, managed to watch the entire procedure, but had to skip the next couple of meals. Luckily she was planning to go into dermatology and not surgery. Allie didn't have any problems, but she had worked for me in my practice at home and had already witnessed lots of dog castrations. The station manager was a young man, and he busied himself at the other end of the kitchen during the surgery. Barbara, or course, had assisted me with many surgeries previously and was my primary assistant for this surgery, too. Pedro woke up nicely following his surgery and just took a couple of extra naps that day. I left instructions for him to be kept out of the canal for a week, until his incision healed.

The next morning we took off in the row boat to look for monkeys, sloths and snakes in the trees and other wildlife along the shore. I've been told there were also large spiders in the trees, but I specifically chose not to look for them and instructed my shipmates not to point them out to me. I don't treat arachnids (spiders), and I'm not interested in them, because, well, I'm afraid of them. When our little tour boat was about ten yards from the dock, we heard a splash. We looked back to see if a giant Cayman was on its way to devour us, but it was only Pedro, who apparently wanted to go sight-seeing, too. We turned the boat around, coaxed him back to shore and tied him up before recommencing our trip. Luckily, his incision healed well and there were no ill effects from his swim.

I Even Treat Worms

After we returned from Costa Rica, we discovered that Barbara had smuggled home a pet, one that I subsequently named Traveler. He was a worm, and he was in her foot, just below the skin. As a vet, I expect to treat (for) worms in animals, but I refused to help Connie out of her predicament. Fortunately, the life span of a worm is short, and Traveler expired of natural causes about ten days later.

Most of the worms I deal with are of the gastrointestinal type. That is, they are worms that are found in an animal's digestive tract. When Allie was taking a parasitology class in medical school, one of the many lovely stories she told me was one about eye worms in people. I had seen only one dog, a yellow Labrador Retriever named Jethro, with eye worms, and that was when I was first out of vet school. It was an incidental finding during a routine exam prior to giving Jethro his vaccinations. While it was very exciting for me, it was not so exciting for Jethro.

The weekend after talking to Allie about eye worms, I got a call from a Sharon Rockford saying that she had just removed a worm from her Weimeriner Zigfried's eye. What a coincidence! She brought Zigfried in and on examination I found and removed two more worms. It felt a bit like a magician reaching up his sleeve and pulling out a string of colored scarves, only I was reaching in poor Zigfried's eye socket and pulling out stringy worms. Again, it was very exciting for me and for my staff, but not particularly exciting for Sharon and even less so for Ziegfried. He has had at least three more eye worms removed in the last year. How or why he became infested by eye worms, I have not been able to determine. I am confident, however, that Zigfried desperately hopes I don't talk to Allie about any other unique parasites or ailments that he could subsequently demonstrate for me.

Pro-Longed Procedure

Boa constrictors are fairly commonly kept as pets. They are often bought at the pet store as eighteen-inch-long babies. The new owner often has no idea that their new baby will grow to twelve feet long! Boas bear live young, so you would expect their deliveries to be pretty uneventful. After all, a twelve-foot, forty-pound snake should have no trouble at all delivering thirty or so skinny little eighteen-inch snakelets that are skinnier than your pinkie. Wrong. Boa constrictors "lay" many eggs that develop inside their uterus. These eggs then "hatch" while still inside the uterus and the baby snakes are then "delivered" into the outside world. But sometimes those eggs may be infertile or don't hatch for some other reason. Now, instead of trying to deliver a long, skinny (one-half inch diameter) little snake, momma snake has to deliver a two-inch-diameter, soft-shelled egg out the same opening. Ouch!

Priscilla was a common boa constrictor. She lived at a local wildlife center in a large exhibit with several other snakes. One of those other snakes was Jesse, a very handsome male boa constrictor. Jesse and Priscilla had been "roommates" for several years and it seems that their relationship was not always platonic.

Priscilla didn't eat for three months. She was looking fat, but she was much more sluggish than usual. Yes, if you know your snakes, you can tell if they are sluggish. Joan, Priscilla's handler, knew that big snakes typically eat only once per week and will not eat for three months while hibernating in the winter, but it was April and the snakes were not hibernating. There did not appear to be any relationship problems with Jesse, so Joan ruled out heartache and angst and decided to bring Priscilla to my clinic for a checkup.

After a thorough examination – palpating the length of a twelve-foot snake takes a while – I decided to take some x-rays. Even with Priscilla coiled up, it took several x-ray plates to get all of her in the pictures. Her sluggish demeanor helped, as normally, restraining a snake for an x-ray is quite a challenge. Once the films were developed, I put them up on the viewer. At first it looked like she had eaten dozens of mice, but Joan was certain Priscilla hadn't eaten in the past three months. On closer examination, all the little skeletons I was seeing in Priscilla's abdomen were actually baby snakes. Priscilla and Jesse had created a huge family, but it was not being delivered as it was supposed to be.

We discussed the options. We could wait some more and hope she went into a normal labor, or I could do a Caesarian section. We decided on the surgical solution.

My surgery room was small, only nine feet wide and ten feet long. My surgery table was five feet long, but Priscilla was twelve feet long. We put most of her body in a snake bag but held her head out of it. We put a mask over her head and anesthetized her with isoflurane, a gas anesthetic. Once she was asleep, I put a tube into her windpipe so we could control her level of anesthesia for the duration of the procedure. She was then laid on her back and taped to a twelve-foot-long two-by-four that was extended diagonally across the room. I had to do a limbo dance to get to the other side of the surgery room, but the patient was secure. Barbara, my assistant, was in one corner of the room at Priscilla's head, monitoring anesthesia. I was near the opposite corner doing the surgery.

Priscilla's uterus was about five feet long, but I certainly wasn't going to make a five-foot-long incision. I made a six-inch incision near the end of the uterus and removed several infertile eggs and several live babies. I was able to remove everything that was in the last eighteen inches or so of the uterus by milking the eggs and baby snakes down to my incision. The rest of the babies and eggs that were further up in the uterus would have to be delivered by Priscilla in the traditional manner. Hopefully I had removed the "plug" so that she could start pushing them out naturally. A snake's uterus is very thin and friable, so I carefully sutured the uterine wall closed and then sutured the skin closed over that. I hoped it would be able to take the stress of more labor. We took Priscilla off anesthesia and down to the recovery room.

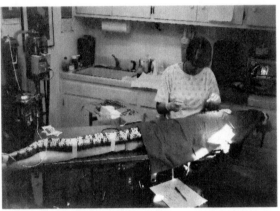

Preparing for a "long" surgery on Priscilla, the twelve-foot boa constrictor.

The recovery room in this instance was the bathroom in my house. I had turned up the heater in the bathroom prior to starting the surgery, so the room was very nicely warmed by the time Priscilla arrived. We laid her on a blanket in the corner and put her three live babies in a box in the other corner. When we checked on her about thirty minutes later, there was another new little baby being delivered. Over the next couple of hours, she had ten more babies and another eight eggs, all delivered as Mother Nature intended. Priscilla and her babies all did very well and she and Jesse added even more to their family two years later.

Micro-Surgery

It wasn't long after the struggle to accommodate twelve-foot-long Priscilla in my surgery suite that I was faced with the opposite problem. We have a terrific exhibit of lizards and quail at the zoo. The majority of the lizards were thriving in the exhibit, as we were regularly finding baby lizards. These lizards were obviously being supplied with an excellent environment that was suitable for breeding and laying and hatching eggs.

Lily, a female collared lizard, was a notable exception. She was fat and obviously pregnant. That should have been a good thing, but she didn't lay her eggs and was not eating well. We watched her carefully for a couple of days, hoping the problem would resolve itself naturally, but she did not improve, remaining fat and unhappy. I started by confirming my diagnosis, taking an x-ray which showed that she was indeed carrying eggs and that they were ready to be laid. Occasionally we can induce "labor" in lizards, but it usually requires providing the perfect environment. Drugs don't work well.

Since Lily already had the right environment, I performed a Caesarian section on her. Lily weighed all of twenty-five grams (slightly less than one ounce!) and was barely four inches from her nose to the base of her tail. I think she is still the smallest animal I have ever done abdominal surgery on. I "delivered" twelve eggs and removed her uterus so we wouldn't have a repeat of this problem. She tolerated the surgery very well, and the entire procedure went surprisingly smoothly from anesthesia to closing the incision. What turned out to be the hardest part of the whole process was removing the drape after the surgery. I usually use a green cotton drape around the surgical field, but with such a tiny patient, it would have covered all of Lily, leading my technician Lucy to complain that she would not be able to see her patient while I was operating. As she was responsible for monitoring the depth of anesthesia while I was operating, I acquiesced and used a clear plastic drape with a sticky backing to make it easier to observe Lily during surgery. When we went to remove the drape after surgery, we found that her feet and legs were stuck to the plastic. The sticky backing that had seemed like such a bright idea at the time was now a problem. The adhesive is only slightly stronger than on a Post-it note, but on such a tiny patient, that's significant. We spent almost as much time carefully prying her toes off the drape as we did performing the surgery, but all her limbs and tiny toes were intact and uninjured when we finished. Lily started eating within two days and doesn't have to worry about having difficulty laying eggs ever again. Best of all, she still has all her fingers and toes and no broken bones!

Knowing When to Refer

One of the nice features of practicing in Southern California is that there are many other vets with whom to consult. There are times when I think a second opinion is in the best interest of the patient and the client, and sometimes it is nice to bounce my thoughts off of a colleague. Other times, I simply enjoy having someone with whom to commiserate over frustrating cases (or clients). The large pool of veterinarians also provides me with someone to whom to refer when I'm on vacation (many of my clients know I like to vacation a lot), to perform procedures I simply don't like performing or when I feel the other vet is superior, or at least more experienced, in a specific subject.

On a Friday afternoon, the day before I was to leave on a week-long family vacation, Alice Jones came in with Veronica, her black pot-bellied pig. Veronica was four years old – full-grown for a pot-bellied pig. She had suddenly started getting very fat – even for a pig – despite the fact that she wasn't eating very well. After doing some diagnostic procedures, I decided that Veronica had a pyometra, an infected uterus, and needed to be spayed. Because she weighed approximately 140 pounds, I was not willing to tackle the surgery by myself. Besides, I was leaving on a week's vacation the next day and would not be around for post-surgical follow-up. This case hit all three of my triggers for referral – imminent vacation, a procedure I didn't (and still don't) like doing, and a large animal. I called my good friend, Dr. Cook, explained Veronica's diagnosis and my circumstances, and he graciously agreed to do the surgery the following Monday.

When I returned the next week, I called Dr. Cook to confirm that my diagnosis was correct and to see how the surgery had gone. Indeed, Veronica's uterus had been infected and had weighed thirty-five pounds! A normal uterus weighs less than one pound. Dr. Cook, who specializes in large animals, such as horses and cattle, said he'd never seen such a large uterus, even in a cow. He had needed to call in another veterinarian to help with the surgery. Jokingly, he told me I owed him my first-born child for that particular referral. I laughed and told him it was a good thing he hadn't sent me that invoice during my vacation. Allie was a wonderful child, but there was a day during our trip when I would have gladly made Quin an only child. Dr. Cook forgave my debt for sending him the referral, Allie remained a member of my family, and Veronica recovered wonderfully, settling back to a svelte 110 pounds and eating well.

The Weather Outside is Frightful

Lynn Weatherby raised Salukis, a breed of dog that is a member of the sighthound family, that is, they hunt by sight rather than by scent. They are tall and slim, looking somewhat like long-haired greyhounds, but they generally have a relaxed demeanor. One of Lynn's finest breed bitches was Tara, a two-year-old with a brown, tan and cream coat. Tara loved to play fetch, but wasn't too keen on surrendering whatever she had retrieved, not atypical of many dogs. While as energetic as any two-year old dog, she definitely fit the "relaxed demeanor" description. Apparently, she had read beyond that brief description of her breed, though, and learned that Salukis are known as "the royal dog of Egypt" and are one of the oldest known breeds of domesticated dog. Tara took her royal lineage to heart and refused to go outside when it was raining, apparently deeming it beneath her station.

Tara had been bred to the top-ranked Saluki in the nation, and Lynn was expecting some outstanding puppies. Naturally, Tara waited to start her labor until a particularly cold and nasty March afternoon when it was pouring rain. She was an indoor dog, and Lynn had a spacious whelping pen in a comfortably heated room, so this shouldn't have presented a problem. This was

Tara's first litter, however, and coupled with the large stud-fee, Lynn was worried. Tara had been in labor for several hours and no puppy had been born, so Lynn decided to bring her to my clinic. Getting Tara into her van was no problem, as Tara loved to take road trips. Besides, it was in the garage, so she didn't have to venture into the harsh outside weather. From the parking lot to my clinic was a different story. Tara was waiting anxiously at the door of the van as Lynn walked around, but when the door opened and Tara saw the rain, she plopped back down and would not budge. Nobody at my clinic was strong enough to carry an expectant Saluki, so rather than jerry-rig a trolley or manhandle Tara, I grabbed my doctor's bag of instruments and climbed into the van to examine Tara. She looked fine to me and I thought her labor was proceeding normally, so I suggested that Lynn take her home because they only lived five minutes away, and I felt they would both be more comfortable waiting there.

In spite of my reassurances, Lynn was far more nervous than first-time mother Tara and was expecting the worst. She simply sat in back with Tara and slid the door of the van closed, remaining in my parking lot, and I went back up to my office. An hour later, between patients, I pulled on my rain poncho and walked down to the van to check on the girls. Tara had routinely delivered a healthy baby girl. Lynn was happy and quite relieved, but decided that they were going to stay there for a while longer. It was still pouring rain. By the end of my office hours, Lynn and Tara went home with three beautiful bitch puppies. Everyone was happy. Was it worth sitting in a car in the rain while your dog whelps? Lynn and Tara thought so.

Sick and Tired of Company

Some cases are easy to diagnose and easy to treat while others are easy to diagnose and hard to treat. Still others are really hard to diagnose but give you a real sense of accomplishment when you finally solve the problem. Then there are those cases that you never diagnose, but resolve themselves anyway.

One of these instances occurred with Jan, a female Barbados Sheep. To many people, Barbados Sheep look like goats rather than sheep as they have hair instead of wool. The Barbados breed is very striking, with a black belly, legs, chest and chin, and a light tan to dark mahogany body. Their faces are often lighter with black stripes. Jan, a tan version, was a very personable, very spoiled ewe who was part of the Smith family. She was treated and acted more like the family dog than livestock. No doubt, Jan lived the good life. One of her favorite activities was to accompany the Smiths on their daily neighborhood walks. She followed them "like a little lamb," not even needing a leash. (Alas, Mrs. Smith's name was not Mary.) Jan was always happy to stop and visit with neighbors and contentedly let little children love on her.

Since they both worked and were away from the house most of the day, the Smiths, Dan and Cynthia, thought Jan would be even happier if they got her another sheep as a companion. They were diligent "parents," so they had read several books on sheep, and they all said that sheep are flock animals and do not do well as single animals. So they bought another Barbados Sheep from the auction at the summer 4H fair and brought it home to live with Jan. Now, they would take both sheep on walks, but the new one, Daisy, had to be on a lead rope.

Very shortly after Daisy joined the family, Jan started some abnormal behaviors on their outings. She would drop her head and refuse to walk and sometimes would collapse to the ground. She showed similar uncharacteristic behaviors at home in their corral. She was still eating, but just wasn't herself.

The Smiths brought Jan in to see me and I did a complete physical examination on her including blood work. The physical exam was relatively normal, but the blood tests did show a very high white blood cell count, so I put her on antibiotics to stop the infection – wherever it was. Over the next couple of weeks, the blood count didn't improve and neither did Jan. I was considering sending her out for an MRI to check for a possible brain abscess or tumor. Before recommending such an expensive procedure, and since the behavior changes occurred after the introduction of Daisy into her life, we decided to try a vacation from the new sheep first. Daisy was sent to a friend's house down the street for a week and Jan was once again an only child. Jan was perfect for the entire week - no unusual behavior at all.

Needless to say, we didn't do the MRI. Daisy found a new home and Jan never again exhibited abnormal behaviors. Although I didn't repeat the blood work, I would almost guarantee that her white blood cell count is perfectly normal now. Jan clearly liked being the center of attention and did not like sharing the spotlight.

Shot in the Hand

Veterinary medicine is a fairly safe profession. There is always a risk of getting bitten or kicked, but by carefully handling and properly "reading" animals, the risk is minimized. Sometimes I managed to injure myself by doing stupid things, which is a danger in any profession.. This was one of those times.

Michael Harker brought in Jessie, one of his older Nubian does. She had produced several very nice kids over the years, but being past prime breeding age, she had been "retired" for several years. This particular morning he had noticed a lump up high on the back of her udder. Since he wasn't milking her anymore, he didn't know how long it had been there, admitting it could have been a couple of months or more. I examined her and thought the lump was an abscessed lymph node. To verify my diagnosis, I stuck a big needle into the lump and tried to aspirate some of the contents into a syringe.

Nothing appeared in the syringe, so I figured some tissue or pus was stuck in the bore of the needle. I disconnected the needle from the syringe, sucked some air into the syringe and reconnected it. Then I pushed hard on the plunger to expel whatever was in the needle. Normally, I aim the needle at a clean surface so I can see what comes out, but I was standing in the center of the goat pen and there were no readily available clean surfaces around. So, like a fool, I aimed the needle at my palm. I would be able to see what was expelled very easily since my palm was clean. Can you see it coming?

As it turns out, the pus inside the needle was very thick and the needle was not tightly attached to the syringe.

Instead of ejecting the pus from the needle, the entire needle came flying off the syringe and implanted itself into the palm of my hand. Ouch! If you've been reading from the beginning of this book, ha ha, I did not pass out. In hindsight, even I'm a little surprised at that.

I simply pulled the needle out of my hand, and this time I *firmly* reattached it to the syringe. I moved to an area with a clean, hard surface (i.e., not my hand) and pushed on the syringe again. This time a thin stream of pus was easily – too easily – expelled from the bore of the needle. I knew immediately that some of that pus was now in the palm of my left hand.

So now I had two reasons to send a sample of the pus to the lab to be cultured – Jessie's health… and my own. I needed to know what bacteria were growing so I could properly treat Jessie, and I figured my doctor could use the same information to treat me. While the lab was processing its culture sample, my hand was busy processing its own – two fingers were swollen and quite sore. I couldn't close my hand to make a fist, so reluctantly but not unexpectedly, I went to see my doctor. I told him the story of how I came to be infected and was also able to give him the Jessie's lab results. He commented that my lab's results were presented much more clearly than those from his lab. I laughed politely, but was more interested in fixing my hand than in helping him find a new laboratory. I told him the bacteria was sensitive to Enrofloxacin, a drug only approved for dogs and cats. He knew that Ciprofloxacin, approved for humans, was in the same class of antibiotics. So he prescribed Cipro, and ten days later I was healed. I have never since aimed a needle at my own hand when examining aspirates, although I must admit that I have come close. Oh, and Jessie was fine after ten days of antibiotics, too.

Wiley Coyotes

Coyotes have lived in the Orange Park Acres (OPA) area far longer than humans have, probably since long before the area was a giant commercial orange grove. New homes and developments have extended beyond the former orange grove and are encroaching deeper into the coyotes' long-established territory. Complicating the situation, thinking they are being kind, many local people put food out for them. So, we should not be surprised that the coyotes are becoming continuously braver and more brazen, trotting down the street in the early mornings and late evenings. Nor should we be surprised they have figured out that it is a lot easier to catch a domestic cat or small dog than it is to catch a wild rabbit or quail. In my twenty-five years in OPA, I lost three cats that just didn't come home. I assume that all three were caught by coyotes. I regret that it took me so long, but after the third loss, I wired in a patio so my cats could still have fresh air and sunshine, without the risk of becoming coyote food.

Her Luck Ran Out

Susie Anderson and Annie, her six-year-old little Yorkshire Terrier, were creatures of habit. Susie was in her mid-fifties, widowed a year after her husband Al gave her Annie as a fiftieth birthday present. She had a job she loved and several animals, but clearly had a special bond with Annie. Each morning started when the alarm went off. Annie would crawl under the covers for a few minutes of cuddling, but only a few minutes. After she had her fill of petting, Annie would wriggle back out and lick Susie's face until she got up, because that would lead to the next point on Annie's agenda – breakfast! The morning routine was completed by a walk around the neighborhood, with Annie racing from tree to bush to fire hydrant, checking up on the latest doggie news while Susie finished waking up with the aid of freshly-brewed coffee. After their walk, Annie was left to guard the house while Susie would head to work. Annie had the run of the house and a dog door leading to an enclosed yard right next to the house.

Bedtime had its own rituals, which started with making the rounds of the outside animals – her three horses and Billy, a male Pygmy Goat. This was Annie's opportunity to explore the rest of Susie's acre of land, having been restricted to her small yard – from which she could see everything, but couldn't get at it – during the day. On this particular night, Susie had just left the barn, on her way to check on Billy, when she heard a commotion in the bushes. Worried that Annie might be after a raccoon or possum, either of which could hurt her badly, or even worse, a skunk, she used her stern, commanding voice while yelling for Annie. The little dog was usually very obedient, but she did not respond to the call. It took Susie almost fifteen minutes of searching in the light of the half moon before she nearly stepped on Annie lying at the back side of the hedges surrounding the barn. Even in the dim light, Susie could see that she had multiple wounds involving her chest and rear legs.

I was doing paperwork in my office that evening and heard the answer machine pick up. After hours, I had a recording that gave the number of an emergency clinic, but would also accept incoming messages. If I was around, I could monitor those messages. Susie was aware that I often monitored the machine, so she started leaving a distress message. As soon as the nature of the emergency became clear, I picked up and told her to bring Annie over. Annie was a lucky dog because none of the wounds were mortal, and I was able to patch her up nearly as good as new. She was going to have several scars, but when her fur grew back they wouldn't be visible. Susie was greatly relieved, but mildly disappointed that her plan to have Annie bred two days later would have to be scrapped (Annie probably wouldn't be in the mood). We surmised that the smell of her being in season slowed the coyote down just enough that he didn't grab her and carry her off before Susie scared him off. Annie healed well, rewarding Susie for her excellent care with a litter of pups the next cycle.

When a cat is caught by a coyote, it is usually eaten. When a dog is caught, it often survives, although small dogs fare worse than large ones. Susie and Annie were lucky she had survived her coyote attack, but Billy, the Pygmy Goat was not so fortunate. He had been a member of the family for eight years and lived in a large pen below the horse barn. Juan Lopez came once a week to help Susie clean the horse area and to do other chores around the property. Some fierce Santa Ana winds broke loose a huge section of a eucalyptus tree, and it came crashing down next to the barn and Billy's pen. When Susie discovered it the next morning, she was immensely relieved it had not fallen a little bit one way or the other, or it might have come down on Billy or the barn. She decided to make good use of the fallen section of tree and had Juan cut it up into firewood, looking forward to its sweet smell in her fireplace. Juan worked diligently the entire day, completing the job by stacking the new firewood neatly along side the goat pen. Sadly, he and Susie were unaware that this gave the coyotes a perfect ramp up into the goat pen. In the middle of that very night, Susie heard the goat screaming. She raced out in only her nightgown, yelling loudly, accompanied by a wildly barking Annie. She saw the coyote hop the fence and scamper away, but it had already "ham strung" Billy. The goat had lost the function of his rear legs and could not stand; So, sadly, we had to euthanize him.

Another Use for Bottled Water

The dolphins I cared for were provided excellent facilities, but the size of the tank and the diversity of life certainly didn't rival the ocean. All the dolphins were born and raised in captivity, so they didn't know what they were missing – great, wide open spaces; sharks, Orcas and other predators; and the need to find and catch their own meals. Another side effect of living alone in something smaller than the Pacific Ocean was that there were no full-time maids. While the human staff tried its best, it could not keep up with the gradual buildup of algae and other debris. If you've ever had a fish tank at home, you get the picture; only this was on a much larger scale. The dolphin pool had to be cleaned and undergo minor repairs about once a year. That meant the pool had to be drained, leaving a not-so-ideal environment for dolphins. The work was done in winter, when there were fewer park visitors to disappoint, and the dolphins were moved to temporary quarters for the several weeks required to complete the pool rehabilitation.

When maintenance time came in mid-January 1994, they were moved to another theme park that had two dolphins of its own. If you lived in Southern California at that time, you may recall a little incident known as the Northridge Earthquake, a shaker that reached 6.7 on the Richter scale. It didn't strike in the middle of the World Series, as the 1989 Loma Prieta (San Francisco) Earthquake did, nor did it cause a bridge to collapse (the Oakland Bay Bridge), but it actually caused more damage, injuries and deaths than its more famous cousin to the north. It was centered very near the other theme park and struck just a few days after our dolphins had been relocated there. That park suffered extensive damage, including cracks in the dolphin pool and the loss of all electricity; not only was water leaking, but that which remained was not being filtered. Not good. All the dolphins, along with their friends the sea lions, had to be moved. They could not survive in unclean water and would do worse (if that's possible) once all the water had leaked out.

The pool at our park, while undamaged by the earthquake, had already been drained and repairs were underway. The maintenance crew, along with several of the animal care staff worked around the clock to get the pool ready for the dolphins to return. Meanwhile, other trainers and I mobilized a large crew to escort the animals home by truck.

Dolphins are mammals, not fish, so they breathe air and can stay out of the water, but it is stressful, and they must be kept wet to stay cool. Whenever we moved them, they rode in special slings hanging over a crate of water. We would half submerge their slings and continuously wring sponges full of water over them. Keeping them in slings was akin to humans using seatbelts. That's what we had done for the trip up to the park, but there was no running water after the earthquake, and thus no way to fill the small tanks in the truck. Despite this challenge, but they had to be moved.

We managed to catch the dolphins quickly, but without water they were going to heat up way too fast in their slings and would not survive the long ride. Lots of ideas – mostly bad ones – were bantered about, until the youngest, least senior park employee had the idea of raiding the concession warehouse. It was just a couple hundred yards down the service road, so we hustled down to see what we could find. The park manager, who was overseeing our efforts, opened the door, and the first things we were greeted with were pallets full of bottled water – tiny, eight-ounce bottles of water, the kind sold to park visitors for an unseemly price. Nobody focused on the lost revenue, though, as they were literal lifesavers. We loaded as many as we could fit into the truck and opened case after case of small bottles and poured them over the dolphins for the four-hour drive. They did the job, and all the dolphins made it safely. I've often thought that we should have taken a picture of someone holding one of the water bottles over a dolphin. I'm sure the water company would have paid a bundle to be able to use it for a commercial on how they helped save the dolphins. I imagined them using a phrase like, "another use for bottled water" or "bottled water for bottle noses." Yeah, I know, I better not give up my day job.

Diaper Gymnastics

Picture yourself changing a baby's diaper. Go on, really picture it! Engage all your senses. First, there is the overpowering foul odor, which means you have to deal with the toxic mess that produced the smell. Then, as if conquering those tasks weren't enough, there is the battle of applying a clean diaper to a squirming mass of freakishly limber arms and legs. Now, add an eighteen-inch tail into the mix. And this is not spindly whip-like tail, but rather one that starts out as thick as the body. How do you get the diaper around both legs and the tail? Most of us have never faced that problem.

The keepers of Princess, a thirty-pound white-throated Monitor lizard, did have to reckon with this conundrum. Big lizards lay on their bellies all the time. Princess had a large outdoor enclosure with large branches for her to climb and bask in the heat-lamp and a low area with a special reptile heating pad for the days when she didn't want to climb. Whereas the heat-lamp heated her from above, working on her heavily-scaled back from a distance, the heating pad was in direct contact with her more tender belly. It was relatively new, but it must have developed a short circuit in its internal wiring because it developed a very hot spot right in the center, leaving Princess with a severely burned belly in the region between her hind legs. Apparently she didn't sense that the pad was getting too hot and move off of it. I guess reptiles are similar to their amphibian relative, the frog. You know, if you put a frog in boiling-hot water, it will jump out, but if you put it in luke-warm water and slowly heat it to a boil, it will remain there until … you reach in and save it.

Princess didn't look happy even before we put her in diapers. Then again, Monitor Lizards *never* look happy.

Anyway, Princess' burn needed to be kept clean and protected, and antibiotic ointment needed to be kept on the wound. This was going to be tough, as she always lay on her belly, either in the dirt, on a tree limb, or on her new heating pad. Furthermore, since lizards have such tough skin, they heal much more slowly than humans do, so the keepers were going to have to treat the wound and, ha ha, monitor the Monitor for several months. We decided that a diaper was the best way to keep ointment on and to protect her belly, but how do you diaper a thirty-pound lizard with an eighteen-inch-long tail? After a few failed attempts that quickly left Princess "naked," her keepers devised a way to diaper her, but had to custom make the diapers. They couldn't use Pampers. They changed diapers and treated the wound daily for a while and every other day for several months. They became quite skilled at the task, and Princess did recover fully, even seeming to wear her diapers regally.

Lump in Her Belly and One in My Throat

Over the years, Sarah became the official greeter for the veterinary clinic. Her 10 x 10 x 20-foot wire cage sat just behind the fence at the top of the driveway, putting her in plain view of everyone that came toward the house or clinic and them clearly in her sights. She would gleefully chatter at everyone that approached, but had special greetings for her closest friends – those that chose to make silly sounds back at her or those that were allowed to go behind the fence to cuddle with her through the wire mesh. She was also known to hold a grudge. If one of her favorite people, Mikey for example, failed to greet her properly, she would shun him on his next couple of visits. She got over it fairly quickly, though, as she simply loved to interact with people.

There were times when her enthusiasm would be short lived or completely absent, such as if she had just been fed. At those times, she might manage a few squeals, but they were probably as much in delight at a raisin or grape she came upon as it was at the person's presence. Other than at mealtime, such quiet or indifferent spells were rare. Thus, by the time she had reached the age of twenty eight, I was pretty well aware of her habits, and

I noticed she had been quieter than normal for several days.

When I fed her in the morning, I almost always made time to hold and cuddle her, taking the opportunity to casually check her over as she groomed me, looking for fleas or other tasty bits in my hair. I was a bit alarmed when she first did this and continuously made little munching sounds. I thought she was finding a treasure trove of juicy delights, but I watched her perform the same ritual on others and was relieved to observe that she made the sound not while extracting edibles, but only in apparent anticipation. Anyway, although I casually inspected her almost daily, I hadn't restrained her for a real physical examination in years. It was clearly time for such an examination and I would have to tranquilize her to accomplish it.

Barbara came and helped me. Sarah's general condition was very good. Her coat was in excellent shape. Her eyes were free of cataracts. Her heart beat loud and strong. Her lungs were clear. Her abdomen was … blast … not fine. When I palpated it, I felt an abnormal mass. Since she was already anesthetized, I chose to go ahead and do exploratory surgery, saving her the stress of a second knock-down. My external findings were confirmed. She had a large tumor involving her uterus. I did a complete ovariohysterectomy, but I was unable to get the entire tumor, as it involved too much of the surrounding tissue.

My expectations, and fears, were confirmed when the biopsy came back fibrosarcoma - cancer. Damn! I wasn't surprised, but I was very discouraged. Actually, I was more than discouraged; I was totally demoralized, verging on devastated. She'd been a part, a big part, of my life for all of her twenty-eight years. I asked a local veterinarian that specialized in surgery if she would be willing to try to do a more complete removal of the tumor. I sent lots of tough surgeries to Linda, so she agreed to help me with Sarah. Barbara went with me, more for emotional than technical or clinical support. Barbara and I got Sarah out of her travel cage and anesthetized. Then we turned her over to Linda and her staff for the surgical procedure, although I did scrub in to observe. Sadly, the tumor had already metastasized. Even Linda's superb surgical skills would not be sufficient to remove it all, so we just closed the incision. I took her home to recover, knowing her days were numbered, just not sure how large that number was.

Which Channel Would You Like to Watch?

Sarah got to live in a cage in the family room for her first post-operative week. She was no dumb monkey, and she quickly learned to play the sympathy card. She would only eat her favorite, special foods, and even then, only if I hand fed them to her. Rotten – I loved her so much – monkey!

At the time, I was working one day a week at another clinic, so I was away most of the day. Still eating only a small amount at each meal, Sarah couldn't be left all day without being fed. Conveniently, Allie, now twenty-five years old, happened to be home from medical school for the week. Not so convenient, though, was the fact that Allie knew Sarah didn't like her, so she was reluctant. Maybe she was beginning to accept the responsibility that came with her chosen profession or perhaps it was just the evil stare I gave her when she balked at my request, but she agreed to feed Sarah.

She – Allie, not Sarah – called me at work later that day and said that she had heated a frozen fettuccini alfredo meal and had fork-fed it to Sarah. She had to hold each bite right up to Sarah's mouth as she reclined on her heated blanket, but if Allie was persistent, Sarah would eat. After over twenty minutes, Sarah had eaten all of the TV dinner. In spite of her initial reticence, Allie seemed quite pleased with herself that she had managed her healthcare duties so diligently and ingeniously, even sacrificing the meal she had marked as her own.

Like Losing a Sister

A year later, when Sarah was twenty-nine and a half years old, I finally had to put her to sleep. The tumor had re-grown to beyond its original size and was impairing her ability to eat and to eliminate. Another surgery in her weakened state would have been risky and arrogant. Sarah had been a marvelous companion, a member of my family, for over twenty-nine years, a very full life for a Spider monkey. It's unlikely she would have survived the surgery, and if she had, it was more unlikely she would ever have regained good health before finally succumbing. As difficult as it was for me, she deserved to go in a dignified and peaceful manner.

I called Allie at school (she was in medical school in Chicago) and tearfully reported what had transpired. I usually withdraw after such sad events, but felt I owed it to Allie to let her know. She later told me what had happened later that day. It made me cry again.

As Allie was leaving her last class of the afternoon, Christine, a close friend and one of her classmates, stopped her and asked if something was wrong, noting that Allie wasn't acting her normal, enthusiastic and outgoing self. Christine peppered her, in a friendly, concerned way, with the usual questions. Was Allie ill? Had she had a fight with Farbod? Had someone died? Allie had quickly rebuffed the first two questions, but faltered at the third. When she explained that her mom's monkey had died, Christine's puzzled look made it clear she didn't understand why that should put Allie in such a funk. Allie somewhat defensively explained, "Sarah was *always* a part of my life. She was like an older sister!"

As Allie finished her story, a huge lump formed in my throat, and a wellspring poured from my eyes. I loved Sarah. I love Allie even more. At that moment, my heart nearly burst.

Learn from Your Mistakes

Stella McIntire was a long-time client of mine. A part-time attorney, full-time mother and marathoner, Stella never had to go out to buy a dog or cat. They just found her, and Stella couldn't say no to a stray. Many of the wayward creatures that found her were not in the best condition, so she would bring them to me for help getting them back into healthy condition. Occasionally she would find a good home for her new pet, but most often it became a member of her ever-expanding household. Stella's fourteen-year-old daughter, Samantha, was an animal lover just like her mom. She not only helped her mom feed and care for the critters, but often added to the family by picking up strays on her own.

Recognizing her love of animals and being very impressed by her enthusiasm and maturity, I hired Samantha to come to my clinic once a week to clean up the facilities. She came at the end of our work day and usually finished after we closed. She was paid for her work, but it certainly was not very stimulating. So, as an additional "perk," I offered to let her volunteer during business hours in the summer. This way, she could have more exposure to the animals and she could watch some of the procedures. When I felt it was safe, I let her hold an animal during my examination, and she could watch surgeries. She never complained about her original job, but she was thrilled to be involved with the real action.

One Tuesday, Samantha came to watch a cat spay. Spays are a pretty clean surgery. I often only get one or two drops of blood on a single gauze sponge during the entire surgery. She intently watched us anesthetize and prep the cat, make the incision and perform the actual surgery. She was very interested and was continually asking really good questions about what I was doing, why I was doing it and what the different internal organs were. I really enjoyed teaching her. As I was starting to close the wound, Samantha's questions seemed to taper off. Merry, my tech that day, noticed too and asked Samantha if she was OK. Samantha feebly responded "Yes" just before we heard a thump as she crumpled to the floor – passed out.

The cat was doing well and I was almost through closing, so Merry was able to go prop Samantha up against the wall and give her a cold cloth to hold on her forehead. By the time I finished and we put the cat in a cage to wake up, Samantha was awake and terribly embarrassed. She was not discouraged, though. She came again the next week to watch another surgery – and was fully prepared with a riding helmet on her head! She never fainted again, but we still haven't let her forget that one time.

Jogging is Good for a Dog's Health

Schatzie was a four-year-old Schnauzer that belonged to Kate Montgomery. Kate lived on the edge of Orange Park Acres with unimproved land (that's "nature" for the world outside of Southern California) across a four-lane street just north of her house. The entrance to her house wasn't off the four-lane road; it fronted on a smaller, parallel lane that was part of a network of small roads that created a cozy, idyllic neighborhood. Or at least so it seemed.

Once you turned off the main road into the neighborhood, you felt like you had been transported into a small community in the countryside, not part of a bedroom community in the middle of Orange County. The back of her property was dominated by a huge grass yard that was about twenty feet above the level of the main road, so you didn't see the road and hardly heard the traffic as you looked out on rolling hills covered by manzanita and scrub brush (California chaparral). That view was what Kate looked forward to every day when she left home long before dawn to commute to her job as a trader on the floor of the Pacific Stock Exchange in downtown Los Angeles. That and the tail-wagging welcome she would receive from Schatzie.

After a hectic day at work, Kate enjoyed sitting on the back patio or, in winter, in front of the sliding glass doors with the fireplace roaring off to her side. She could completely unwind with a cup of chamomile tea or, more often, a glass of fine red wine. She had a boyfriend, Peter, a fellow trader, but they usually only saw each other on the weekend. Schatzie was her shadow when she was home. Kate's appreciation for Schatzie's love was shown with a few too many treats, as I scolded her every time she brought her slightly obese treasure in for her shots.

Apparently I wasn't the only one who noticed how plump Schatzie had become. On one of the rare Saturday mornings when Peter was not at her house, one of her two days a week when she could sleep in past sunrise, she grumbled her way to the front door at 5:30 a.m. after being woken from a sound sleep by persistent loud knocking. Standing on her front porch was some stranger, a handsome, albeit sweaty guy. No way would she open the door to such a person in the wee hours of the morning, except even through the peephole she recognized the bundle in his arms – her Schatzie! What was this guy doing with her dog that was supposed to be asleep in the backyard? As it turns out, Mike Kale, a neighbor from a couple of streets away, had been out for his morning run when he turned the corner to see a coyote carrying Schatzie down the side of the street. He didn't recognize the dog, but he was certain it didn't belong to the coyote, so he yelled and started running after the coyote. Mike said he must have really surprised the coyote, because it jumped straight up in the air, dropped Schatzie, and bolted off into a yard, headed back toward the hills. Mike followed Schatzie home and then knocked on the door to awaken Kate. Schatzie had only a couple of minor puncture wounds and recovered without incident.

When Kate brought Schatzie in and described what had happened, I started to grouse about blasted coyotes coming into backyards to snatch pets. Kate quickly interrupted my rant, explaining that she found a hole by the front gate. Schatzie had always been a notorious digger, and was probably wandering in the street or front yard inconveniently (for Schatzie) at the time the coyote was prowling around in search of breakfast. Kate repaired the hole and started checking the fence frequently. For her part, Schatzie is now convinced that jogging, specifically Mike jogging, is good for her health!

Some Friends You Are!

Romeo, a brown and white Cocker Spaniel, wasn't quite as lucky as Schatzie. At 5:00 a.m., Rick Bryant had let his three dogs outside. He waited at the door, because he knew they would want right back in after they relieved themselves. After all, it was winter, and his dogs were true Southern Californians, considering anything below sixty degrees to be inhumanly (or incaninely) cold. As he stood there waiting, Rick wondered why they couldn't have waited another hour, but the two Labradors, Tom and Jerry, had been whining so loud that he could hear them through the pillow and blankets he had pulled over his head in an attempt to block out the unwelcome early start to his day.

His daydreaming at the back door was interrupted by a bone-chilling yelp that he recognized as Romeo. Any remaining sleepiness was evaporated by a burst of adrenaline, and he raced out to see what the problem was. A coyote had jumped the five-foot-tall fence, grabbed Romeo by the neck, and was making a getaway with his prize, headed back toward the fence. The coyote had a big head start but was forced to let go of Romeo when Rick snatched up a rake and chucked it like a spear at the fast disappearing predator. Rick had been an athlete in high school, but that had been a long time ago. Just the same, he was impressed at how close he had come with his toss, and immensely relieved to have saved Romeo from a gruesome end.

It wasn't all rosy once the coyote had let Romeo go. He had several very deep puncture wounds on his neck that required months of flushing and treatment. He did recover, but even six months later, he would not go out back alone in the dark. Rick had to walk outside with him, which he did willingly, even in the rain. We all wondered why Tom and Jerry hadn't gone to his rescue. They were the ones that raised the cry to go out, probably because they heard or sensed the intruder. Romeo was clearly the alpha dog in the family, continuously nipping at his brothers' heals. Maybe Tom and Jerry sensed an opportunity to get rid of the pesky little guy. Nah, only humans could plan something so dastardly. It's more likely that their bravado ended when they actually came face to face with the coyote.

The Rhea Thing

Rheas are the South American version of the ostrich. They are a smaller bird than an ostrich, typically weighing 65 pounds versus over 200 pounds for an ostrich, but they are similar in color, a mixture of beige, brown, black and gray. While ostriches have the reputation for sticking their heads in the sand, as in they ignore trouble, rheas are considerably more flighty. One day, one of the rheas that I cared for, Rita, was seen being chased by the small herd of guanacos (similar to llamas), Rita's cohabitant compatriots in the South American exhibit. A zoo visitor watched the chase and said she found it entertaining until she noticed that the rhea had some blood up high on her right leg, so she pointed it out to a zoo staff member. Rita's keeper Joannie was concerned that she may have been kicked but could not get a good view of the injured area. Worried that the injury might be serious, Joannie called Barbara, the curator, who in turn paged me. I pulled myself away from whatever project I was engrossed in on that beautiful Southern California summer Sunday afternoon and drove to the zoo.

As I noted earlier, rheas are a very nervous bird, so in order to reduce her mental stress, we tried to check her out from outside the exhibit. Besides being flighty, Rita was also being uncooperative, as she would not stand still and she would not stand in a good position for me to see the inside of her leg. We eventually isolated her in a holding area at the end of her yard, and with lots of keepers lined up we managed to catch her with no injuries to either her or any keepers.

I examined her leg and did not find a wound or any other apparent source of the blood. As I moved up and started examining her wing, I discovered a broken blood feather. I pulled it with only a minor complaint from Rita and immediately cured the bleeding problem. New, growing feathers are called "blood" feathers because the center of the feather shaft is filled with blood to supply nutrients while it is developing. Once the feather is fully formed, the blood withdraws out of the shaft. Apparently, formed feathers no longer require nutrients. Excuse the poor attempt at humor, but the withdrawal of blood also makes it easier to fill shed feathers with ink (for use as quill pens).

Rita wasn't lame and there were no palpable abnormalities of her leg, so I told the holders to turn her loose. They let go and moved away and she tried to get up, but fell right back down. We hadn't given her any drugs for restraint, and we hadn't restrained her very long, but I was still concerned about stress or heat-related problems. We supported her on the ground and she lay there quietly. This is very abnormal for a rhea; they do not tolerate having people close to them. Twenty minutes passed and Rita was still lying quietly on the ground. I gave her several injections for stress and shock, but she still stayed on the ground. I went to get another medication, but she died before I could even administer it. This was a very unexpected and frustrating result of a seemingly innocuous catch-up.

I did a necropsy on her, with the hope of learning something, but I really didn't expect to find an answer to why she died. Animals that die suddenly often do not show any abnormalities on gross examination. But Rita surprised me. I usually talk my way through a necropsy and show all the normal and abnormal findings to whichever keepers are watching. Starting in the chest cavity, I showed them the heart muscle and valves on the left side of the heart and then I opened the right side of the heart. I couldn't find the heart valves. I opened the heart a little more and still couldn't find them. I looked back at the left side – and sure enough, there were the valves. I looked at the right side again but just couldn't find them. I could point right where they should be, but I could not find them. I finally looked up at the keepers who were observing the necropsy and had noticed the pause in my narration and explained my quandary. This was a three-year-old bird. We had caught and restrained her several times previously. If she had no heart valves, then they were missing at birth. How could she live for three years?

I put the heart into formalin and took it out to the California State Veterinary Laboratory and showed it to the veterinary pathologist there. I asked her to show me the right-side heart valves, admitting that I had been unable to find them. She couldn't find them either, so I regained some of my self-confidence, and we were both equally unable to explain how or why Rita had been so normal for three years.

Sometimes Just Watching is Hard

Sassy was a typical Jack Russell Terrier. She thought she owned the world. She considered nobody a stranger and was convinced that all other dogs loved her. Terriers are notoriously energetic, and Sassy was no exception, but she was so loving and friendly that her vivaciousness could never be considered a nuisance. Her accepting nature and anxiousness to greet everyone and everything she saw came back to bite her one day –

literally. While making her morning rounds of the backyard, she met a strange "dog," who turned out to be neither loving nor friendly, unless you consider the teeth the coyote sunk into Sassy's neck and shoulders a love bite. John Gilbert, her dad, heard her terrified cries as he was sipping his morning coffee. He knew there were coyotes in the area, having seen them occasionally when he, his wife, Sally, and Sassy went for early morning walks in the neighborhood. He feared the worst as he ran through the living room to the French doors that led to the back patio, thinking he would not be quick enough to save his little friend. Apparently Sassy managed to fight hard enough that the coyote dropped her, because as he reached the doors, he saw her limping back toward the safety of the house and the back end of the coyote on its way over the fence.

My clinic normally opened at 9:00 a.m., but since my clinic was in my barn, it was not extremely uncommon for clients to show up on my doorstep at odd hours. John and Sassy appeared on my doorstep at the relatively decent time of 7:30. I had been up since 6:30, had already fed all the animals, had my breakfast (a Dr. Pepper) and was doing paperwork in my office, so it was no bother to head up to the clinic with my emergency patient. Sally had come, too, but she was waiting in the car. Not only couldn't she watch this procedure, she couldn't even stay in my exam room when Sassy came in for her annual vaccinations!

Sassy had several nasty bite wounds, but they were clean punctures. There weren't any tears and not any muscle or nerve damage. I cleaned and disinfected the punctures and put drains in a couple of the worst ones. John was a fireman and a paramedic, so wound care was not a problem for him. I have always preferred to send my patients home as quickly as possible since I think they recover more quickly in their own home. John watched me flush the wounds and assured me that he would have no problems flushing them himself. Sassy was a very brave pup for the procedure, too.

Since John was a fireman, he worked for three days straight at the local fire station and then was off for four days. Sassy's treatment went on for several weeks, and the wounds required flushing twice a day. When John was at work, Sally brought Sassy to my clinic for treatment, but there were times my clinic was closed and I was working elsewhere a few days a week. There was no way Sally was going to irrigate the wounds herself, so she would take Sassy and the flushing material to the fire station twice a day so John could do the treatment. Luckily, it wasn't his busy fire season. Sassy healed well, but Sally still leaves the exam room if I have to give Sassy any shots.

Flunked Retirement

A Reluctant Departure

After many years practicing veterinary medicine, I decided to stop, quit practicing, retire. After over twenty-five years of practicing out of my barn, a couple of my neighbors started grumbling about the "traffic" and "all the cars" parked in our cul-de-sac. I started to encourage clients to park in my driveway, but many still parked in the cul-de-sac. Unsatisfied, the neighbors next informed me that my business was illegal and threatened to turn me in to the city if I didn't shut it down. I was dumbfounded. They sure didn't seem to mind having a veterinary practice next door when they knocked on my door in the middle of the night to attend to their sick or injured pets!

I wasn't ready to quit, but I didn't think I could afford to open a "regular" clinic. Plus, I was accustomed to having my pets with me and all the comforts of home merely steps away. In the mornings, I would walk, barefoot of course, from the house up to the barn, and back down for lunch or bathroom breaks. I couldn't fathom the drastic change of driving to work and sitting inside some sterile, windowless box all day, so I convinced myself that retirement was a good idea.

I could sleep in mornings. I could relax and work on stained glass projects. I could travel. OK, I already did travel a ton, but it still sounded good. I wouldn't be responsible for animals' lives and well-being. All combined, it was enough that I officially retired. My friends and clients weren't happy, pleading with me to reopen elsewhere, tugging mightily at my heart strings, but I held firm. For their part, they finally accepted my decision and gave me an awesome retirement party. I felt so incredibly loved and appreciated that day!

Before I even officially closed, I started missing my clients and their pets. In less than a year, my drive to care for animals - and their owners - combined with a growing frustration at how other vets were treating "my" patients, caused me to go back to work. I flunked retirement, and my clients were ecstatic. I started working two afternoons a week at a colleague's veterinary clinic. Word traveled quickly. My old clients flocked back, completely filling my schedule. Several were a bit worried upon their first visit to the new clinic. I was wearing shoes, and that just didn't seem right to them. About a year later, I succumbed to the pressure of my clients and my shoes and reopened Quillie Acres Veterinary Clinic in a strip mall and got back to practicing barefoot.

After five years, I've retired again and hope to be successful this time.

No More Pups!

I suppose all professionals have their embarrassing moments at work, but sometimes I think I have had more than my share. I am surprised that I'm admitting to some of those mistakes in a book for the whole world to read.

One that left me particularly chagrinned involved a very good friend, Briana Hale, who raised Labrador Retrievers. We first met at the pre-school our children attended. When she found out that I was a veterinarian, she brought one of her puppies to my clinic. She was pleased both with the fine work I did, and with how close my clinic was to her home, so she started using me as her regular vet. Between puppy shots, clipping dewclaws, pregnancy checkups, artificial insemination, the occasional sick puppy or difficult delivery, and of course, pre-school, we met quite often, and our friendship grew strong. When our kids finally started primary school and we both actually had six hours a day without children underfoot, she started working part time for me. We had several long discussions on the concerns of working with a good friend and decided that we could maintain both a friendship and a working relationship. We did that very well, and Briana worked for me for many years before moving a little too far away to justify the commute.

Over those many years, I had talked her through many deliveries and done several Caesarian sections on her dogs. She was an excellent midwife to her dogs. On this particular occasion, Briana called late on a Sunday afternoon because Fiona had started labor but had quit having puppies after just two pups. Briana brought the bitch (that is a polite and proper term for a female dog) over and we prepped her for surgery (a Caesarian section). I didn't need to call in an assistant, because Briana was one. I opened Fiona up and pulled out her uterus. It was empty! There were no more puppies! I felt foolish and I felt like a very bad veterinarian. I should never have started that surgery without verifying that there were more puppies in her, which I could have done by palpating her abdomen, a simple, non-surgical procedure. I knew better and Briana knew better. There is no acceptable excuse for my mistake, but I know I made it because Briana was a good friend, and a knowledgeable dog breeder – and we were busy talking and worrying about the surgery. I just figured there was no reason to argue with her about doing a surgery – if the dog had quit pushing, it must be for a good reason. I neglected to remember that very best reason to stop labor is because there is nothing else to push out. Briana, of course, was laughing "with" me. Fiona did fine with her unnecessary surgery. And I learned another big lesson.

Man Bites Dog

Over the years, I have treated several dogs that have been attacked by coyotes. I've known of many cats that have been attacked by coyotes, but few of them have lived to be treated. But one day, I got a call asking if I would treat a coyote that had been attacked by dogs. I took the phone call because I had to at least hear the story. Not quite "Man Bites Dog," but close.

Marianne Granger boarded Cicero, her golden Palomino at a horse stable in the canyon. The stable owner had two German Shepherds that stayed in a pen at the side of the property. Fritz and Heidi were friendly dogs, but considered it their job to protect the stables. Mid-morning on a Wednesday, her day off from nursing duties at a local hospital, Marianne was grooming Cicero when she heard a commotion in the dog pen. She went to investigate and found a coyote pup in the pen with the two Shepherds. Fritz and Heidi were very agitated and were snapping at the pup, trying to force it to leave. The coyote pup was about six months old and had multiple small bite wounds on his face and legs. He was very frightened and was cowering in a corner, apparently unable to find his way out. Marianne managed to calm Fritz and Heidi enough that she could attach their leashes and tie them to a fence post. Although the dogs were now restrained, they continued to bark and snarl at the coyote, which remained huddled in the corner of the pen. It looked adorable, vulnerable and cuddly, but Marianne knew better than to try to handle a wild coyote, especially a frightened one. She spied a dog crate nearby and pushed it into the corner. The frightened pup seemed to welcome the apparent refuge and scampered into the plastic crate, perhaps imagining it was a magical den that would transport him away from this terrifying situation.

That was indeed Marianne's intention, but now that she had rescued the pup, she was having a lot of difficulty finding a veterinarian who would treat a wild coyote.

I was used to treating exotic animals – actually, I love it – so when her stroll through the yellow pages led her to me, I told her to bring him on into my clinic. By the time she arrived, he was in shock and, if he were human, would have been ready to faint. I asked Marianne what she wanted to do with the little guy. She wanted to release him near where she found him. That pleased me, as I didn't want him to end up in a cage in captivity. We pulled him out of the crate and muzzled him; he didn't put up any fight. I treated his wounds, which were mostly superficial. One cut on his forepaw required a couple of stitches. I used dissolvable stitches, as I did not expect him to come back for any follow-up visits. He was clearly nervous, but still enough in shock that we were able to restrain him and treat him without any anesthetic. I gave him a shot of long-lasting antibiotics, treated him for shock and put him back into the crate. Marianne promised to take him home, keep him in a quiet room for twenty-four hours and then release him.

She called the next day and said that he had a good night. He had drunk some water and eaten the dead mouse that she had put in with him. (I was quite impressed at all the effort Marianne went through for the wild little critter.) He was alert now and aware of her presence, tracking her through the side panels of the crate as she walked by. In the late afternoon she and a friend took the crate and clambered down to the bottom of the hill, a hundred yards or so below the dog pen. She was guessing that this was where he had probably started before getting trapped by the dogs. Reaching carefully from the side, she opened the crate door, expecting the pup to immediately bolt, but he didn't move. Accepting that the coyote might not understand all that she had done was to help him and that he might be frightened of her, Marianne and her friend left the crate with the door open and scrambled back to the top of the hill. About half an hour later, they saw him first peer out and then slink out of the crate. As soon as he was completely out of the cage, he darted off, disappearing into the brush, hopefully toward home and his family. His wounds had been minor and we all hoped that he fared well back in his home territory. Even with the long-lasting antibiotics there was still the chance that his wounds could become infected, but we were all willing to take that chance since it also gave him the chance at a normal life. Hopefully he also learned to stay away from domestic dogs.

Half the Canine She Used to Be

"Penny just pulled her tooth out!" came the panicked voice over the phone. "Relax Donna, and bring her on in" I soothed. I felt sure she had broken the tooth and not pulled it out. A short while later, in walked Penny, a five-year-old nearly-blonde yellow Labrador Retriever, with her right canine tooth dangling from her mouth. It wasn't broken. She was another example of how much tougher than humans (at least me) dogs are. The tooth was hanging just outside her mouth, attached by a strand of gum. It must have hurt, but Penny was a happy, wiggling bundle of energy as she came into the clinic.

As I was inspecting Penny's mouth, I asked Donna if she knew how Penny had managed to pull her own tooth – it was a beautiful extraction; one that I would have been proud to have done. Donna lowered her head and shamefully declared it was her fault. Penny spent her days in a large dog run at the side of the house. When Donna returned from work at the local feed store, her routine was to let Penny out of her pen to join her for a quick dip in their backyard swimming pool. Today, however, Donna had invited a friend and her young son to come over for a swim and worried Penny's exuberance might be too intimidating for the boy. Apparently, in her frustration at being left out, Penny tried to bite through the chain link, caught her tooth and performed the near perfect extraction. Donna knew something was up when Penny's intermittent barks of disappointment and frustration at not being allowed to join the fun were replaced by a piercing yelp followed by a more subdued whimpering. Donna hustled back to check on her best friend, finding her sitting with a somewhat confused look and a very crooked smile. That's when she made her panicked call to me.

By the time her story was complete, I was nearly done with Penny, but let me go back and explain. Below the gums, human canine teeth start the same size as the exposed portion, tapering down to a blunt point as they extend deeper into the gum. In a dog, on the other hand, a canine tooth is a bit like an iceberg. It has a root that is about twice the size of the visible tooth. Extracting a canine tooth on an adult dog can normally be a bit of a challenge. But in Penny's case, there were no obvious fractures of the tooth or the bone that had surrounded it, and the tooth was just hanging by a bit of gum. I anesthetized her, cut through the gum to finish releasing the tooth and then stitched closed the hole that was left behind. Penny healed perfectly – minus one canine that is.

Oh My Aching Back

Rosy was a rosy boa (what else?), one of two members of the boa constrictor family that is native to the United States. Rosy boas are olive green to gray with various colored longitudinal stripes, and are relatively small for boas. Their small size and generally docile nature make them ideal pets (assuming you consider any type of snake could be an ideal pet). Rosy was indeed a very gentle snake and had been used in education programs for a long time. We knew Rosy was a girl because she had laid eggs several different years. Boa babies develop inside an egg, but are born live. Occasionally, even if a female has never had a boyfriend, she will deliver infertile eggs.

Pat Wynn had worked with Rosy for four years, and always held her during public presentations. While showing off Rosy to a group of first graders at a local elementary school, she noticed that the little kids were much squirmier and more flexible than Rosy was. Rosy could not coil up in her hands as she usually did. She would hang awkwardly off the edges of Pat's hands, and Pat was sure she was holding her hands the same as always. Rosy simply could not bend properly. There was a six-inch area in the middle of her body that was rigid. While there is something to be said for developing a backbone, Rosy already had one, as all snakes do. A snake's normally very flexible backbone is comprised of many sections, and the ribs are connected by muscle to the scales on its abdomen. A snake "walks" or slithers by moving its scales. A stiff back is as debilitating for a snake as it is for a human.

When I examined Rosy, I could only agree with Pat's observations. Rosy was a normal, flexible snake except for a six-inch section of her back. I took x-rays, which showed that Rosy had a disease called Osteitis deformans (known as Paget's disease in humans). She had arthritic changes all around the vertebrae in that section of her back, and the arthritic growths had literally fused her back. In humans, fusing is a treatment for some back problems. In this snake, the fusion had over-reacted. Not only was an entire six-inch section of spine fused (in a three-foot snake), but there was a lot of excess calcification on the bottoms of the vertebrae that was infringing on the space in the abdomen. Unfortunately, there is no cure, no way to undo the arthritic growths or the damage they have caused. I read about some drug therapies which would slow the advance, but we realized that, eventually, Rosy would not be able to pass food down her intestinal tract. At the time, she was eating fine, and she was acting normally, so Rosy got to retire from show business. She didn't do any more education programs. She now spent her days (or should I say nights, as boas are nocturnal) kicking back, just eating, sleeping and slithering around her cage.

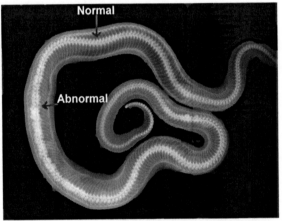

Rosie's x-ray, showing advanced Osteitis deformans (known as Paget's disease in humans). It was no wonder she was uncomfortable.

Rosy had over a year of luxurious retirement before Pat noticed she was very inactive and looked "uncomfortable." (Trust me, knowledgeable people can tell when their snake is uncomfortable.) We had x-rayed her about six months after first diagnosing her ailment, and happily, the disease had not progressed significantly. On this occasion, when I examined her, I found that the fused area of her spine had broken. We never figured out if she had wedged herself improperly in her cage or if a large food item had put too much pressure on the fused area, but the end result was a broken back. While it was not completely unexpected, it was still very disheartening. We euthanized Rosy that day, comforted by the feeling that she had enjoyed her year of retirement.

Those are NOT Toys!

Sean and Molly Jefferson were newlyweds, married a mere three months when it happened. It was a pleasant fall day. They were out for an afternoon walk in a local park they came upon Tiger. Not a wild tiger, rather a young orange and white kitten that they would soon name Tiger. He couldn't have been more than six or seven weeks old. Being alone in this particular park, far from any homes, they figured he must have been abandoned. If he was a feral cat, he hadn't developed any of their normal traits of cautiousness and wariness. Sean first spotted him nestled in a pile of leaves beside the trail, fast asleep.

When Sean pointed the kitten out to Molly, she quietly exclaimed, "Ohhhhhhh, how precious!" and set herself down cross-legged nearby. She softly called out and lightly rustled the leaves nearby. First, an ear twitched, then Tiger raised his head with squinty sleepy eyes looking for what had disturbed his slumber. When he spied Molly sitting nearby, she fully expected him to dart off into the adjacent shrubs. Instead, he stood, a bit unsteadily, stretched mightily with an equally mighty yawn, sat down and stared at Molly. She was sold. He was indeed precious.

Emboldened by his lack of skittishness, she twirled a leaf she was holding, hoping to engage him in play. At about that moment, Tiger seemed to come awake. He opened his mouth wide again, not in a yawn this time, but letting out a pleading mew. He got up and headed directly to Molly, continuing his plaintive cries. She immediately scooped him up and cuddled him against her chest. He responded with loud purring accentuated by continued mewing. They already had a pet, Rufus, Sean's six-year-old Rhodesian Ridgeback dog, but Sean knew instantly that their family had just grown by one.

After a day or so spent mostly behind the couch hissing at the big bad dog, Tiger settled into the household quite nicely. He seemed to figure out that Rufus didn't have a mean bone in his body, and was simply excited and curious to meet his new little brother. Tiger quickly grew to love Rufus and could often be found fast asleep between Rufus' paws – when he wasn't batting at or hanging on the poor, tolerant dog's tail or ears. He was a kitten after all, and kittens love to play. Besides tormenting Rufus, he loved to chase string, climb up furniture (those claws might have to go) lunge after toy mice hanging on springy cords, chase after plastic balls with bells in them, and attack wiggling toes at the bottom of the bed (those claws definitely have to go).

Tiger was as attached to his humans as he was to Rufus. He would follow Sean into the bathroom every morning, peeking in around the shower curtain, squinting and retreating when water spray splashed his way, only to peek right back in. Both he and Sean seemed to enjoy the game. After his shower, Sean would shave before returning to the bedroom to dress. Sometimes Tiger would go back to bed and cuddle with Molly, but he usually stayed with Sean. He could always find something to play with no matter where he was. Kittens are very resourceful. On this particular day, Sean, wrapped in his towel, was leaning over the sink lathering up his face. As Tiger was weaving between Sean's feet, he peered up and spied some dangly objects hanging above him. Figuring these were as-yet undiscovered toys, he leapt up and grabbed them with his claws (those claws have to go NOW). Neither Sean nor Tiger were pleased with the result of playing with those toys.

It was just a few days later that Molly brought in Tiger and I declawed him. A couple of days later, I received a very nice thank-you note from Sean that read "Thanks for saving my privates." Tiger did not send me a note.

Neurosurgeon and Cat

'Twas the Christmas season, and Allie and her fiancé, Farbod, were spending part of their vacation with me. Allie had received her medical degree the previous June and was doing her first year of a radiology residency in Chicago. Farbod was in the third year of his neurosurgical residency at the same hospital. Besides visiting me and Farbod's family in Hollywood, they were planning their April wedding, which was going to be held in the nearby posh beach community of Laguna Beach (It was a beautiful wedding, by the way).

On one of their rare, non-action-packed days, we were relaxing at the breakfast table basking in the overstuffed afterglow of some New Orleans-style beignets, complete with strawberry sauce and powdered sugar, that Allie had prepared. In addition to being smart (she is a doctor), she is a talented artist (when she is so inclined) and an amazingly accomplished chef. If she tastes something she enjoys, she will figure out how to prepare it herself. I know she's my daughter, but I'm still super impressed. But I digress.

Farbod was sipping coffee, Allie some tea, and I was having my usual Dr. Pepper. We were deciding where to go shopping when the phone rang. It was Dorothy Jones, a client who raised Scottish Fold cats, a breed that looks like a cross between an owl and a cat. This is largely because, unique to the Scottish Fold breed, their ears are folded forward and downward on their heads, a result of an incomplete dominant gene. The kittens are born with straight ears, which at three to four weeks, may fold down. They can have straight ears, but they are not considered show quality if they do. Dorothy raised only longhairs, and she was very proud of the quality of her cats. Jasmine, one of her prize queens (female cat) was in season, and she had put Thomas, her best male cat, in with her early that morning. Dorothy was already dreaming of the beautiful kittens Jasmine would be delivering in about nine weeks. Shockingly, about an hour later, when she went to check on the two cats, she found Thomas dead. He had apparently died while breeding the queen. He was only a year old, so Dorothy was anxious to learn why he had died. I told her to bring the cat to my house and I would do a necropsy.

Allie had observed and participated in a lot of necropsies while growing up. I like to think that her years of living with a veterinarian helped her decide to go into medicine, albeit human medicine. Farbod did not have Allie's experience and was very interested in watching the cat necropsy, so they headed over to the clinic with me. There was no gross pathology pointing to the cause of death, but I was suspicious of the heart. When I was done with the examination and had collected samples to send to the lab for blood work, toxicology and tissue analysis, I had to sew up Thomas neatly to return to Dorothy. Even though he was very young, she had grown very attached to him and wanted to bury him in her yard. As I still had to fill out the paperwork for the lab samples, and we still wanted to go shopping, I asked Farbod if he would mind sewing up Thomas. He was very enthusiastic and willing to help me out. As a third year resident, he was still mostly doing scut (go-fer) work and observing, so he was excited to get in and ply his trade, even if it was only "closing," and on a cat, at that. I gave him the suture material and the appropriate instruments and sat down to write up what I had found. Farbod's first comment was, "I don't have to deal with this much hair in my surgeries." He made a very neat and tidy suture line on the cat. It later dawned on me that I should have taken a picture of Farbod while he was suturing. I could have sent a copy to one of his neurosurgery professors so they could see to what good use he was putting his medical training.

And in case you were wondering, nine weeks later we learned that Thomas' death had not been completely in vain. Jasmine delivered seven gorgeous kittens, one of which went on to win "Best of Breed" at a national show.

In Closing

Bud was a typical five-year-old Jack Russell Terrier in that he considered himself a big dog, in spite of standing only ten-inches tall. He and his two-year-old "brother," Blackie, a bundle of energy disguised as a brown and white boxer, lived with their humans, Jim and Jane Gray, in a sprawling, ranch-style home on over an acre of land, adjacent to a hilly, undeveloped section of Orange Park Acres. Although they were considered members of the family, Blackie and Bud slept outside, usually cozying up in their sheepskin beds on the back porch, an over-sized redwood deck that stepped down into a grass yard bordered by orange trees.

Early one foggy June morning, Jim and Jane woke up and went to the back door but were not met by their usual welcoming committee of two furiously-wagging tails, wriggling bodies and gleefully-lolling tongues anxiously awaiting their breakfast. Quite surprised and mildly alarmed, they called and whistled, searched the yard and the garage, but still no dogs. The fencing around the yard enclosed part of the front of the house as well, so they went around to check the front porch and saw Blackie huddled up in a corner. Confused and concerned that Blackie did not bound down to greet them, Jim went up to check on him, and Jane went to make another pass through the backyard. Before she got far Jim called her back, having discovered why Blackie was not moving – he was curled up around and practically on top of Bud. Apparently Bud had been attacked by coyotes during the night and Blackie had protected him. Blackie was uninjured, but Bud had several gaping wounds and was in very bad shape. Even though Blackie had kept him warm, Bud was in shock from the attack and the extent his wounds.

Under normal circumstances, I would have either received a panicked phone call or, as I lived nearby, been awakened by a knock on my front door, but I had closed my practice several months earlier, so Jim and Jane rushed Bud to a local emergency clinic. The staff at the clinic, one that I frequently recommended, provided Bud with excellent care. Jane kept questioning the treatment, however, pointing out that, "Dr. Boldrick would have done it such and such way." In my practice I sent almost all patients home for nursing care. The emergency clinic wanted to keep Bud for several days for observation and ongoing wound treatment. Jane would have no part of that. She let them do the emergency treatments, and said she would bring Bud back as often as they said he needed, but then took him home – against their recommendation – because, "that's the way Dr. Boldrick would have done it."

I am immensely honored that she was happy with my care of her animals, but I don't think the doctors at the emergency clinic were equally impressed. In spite of their concern, Bud healed well and was back to his normal "big dog" self in just a couple of weeks.

While neither the story in the Introduction nor this one correspond precisely with the start or end of my veterinary career, respectively, they are close, and they provide remarkably complementary (and complimentary) bookends for this collection of wonderful memories. I hope you enjoyed reading them as much as I did experiencing them in the first place and reliving them as I wrote about them.

Afterword

Writing this book has brought back a lot of memories - good and sad. As I look back, I realize that I am really happy with my choice of profession. I learned to love medicine from my father, an M.D., but people were never my big concern - animals were. So, I put medicine and animals together and, naturally, selected veterinary medicine. Dad was encouraging of my career choice, but I don't think he was genuinely excited by my decision. Fortunately, I know that both he and Mom ended up being very proud of me. My daughter, Allie, was only two when he passed away, but he would be tickled that she is now a doctor, too. Better yet, from his perspective, she has reverted back to humans. Maybe her daughter will be the next veterinarian in our family?

As my years in practice increased, my concern for my patients did not diminish; rather, it continually increased. It always hurt when I lost a patient, but that pain seems to have grown more intense over the years. I have always tried to practice quality medicine while avoiding a lot of unnecessary tests and procedures. Sometimes I've skipped a test that, in hindsight, should have been performed. But more often, my educated opinion has saved my patient some pain and my client some money ... and turned out right for both.

I've been lucky to have had a lot of quality pet owners. Anyone who would come to a *barn* for a *second* visit was usually the kind of owner with whom I wanted to work. Most of them wanted to be involved in the care and treatment of their pets, and they were quite pleased when I sent them home with follow-up nursing instructions. And, importantly, most of them carried out that nursing care very well. We worked *together* to achieve and maintain the health of their pet.

I lament every mistake I've made, but I know that I never deliberately did a disservice to any patient. I am proud to be a veterinarian. And, in spite of an occasional bruised toe, I feel exceptionally fortunate to also be a *barefoot* veterinarian.

Key to inter-story paws (pauses)

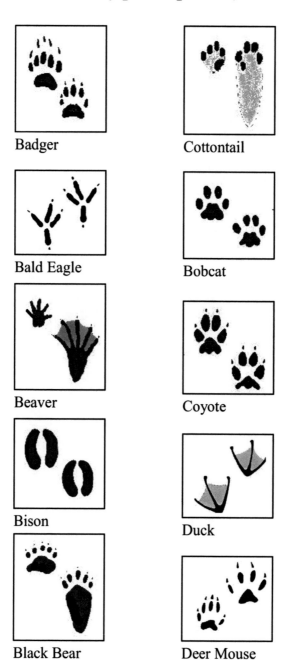

Badger

Cottontail

Bald Eagle

Bobcat

Beaver

Coyote

Bison

Duck

Black Bear

Deer Mouse

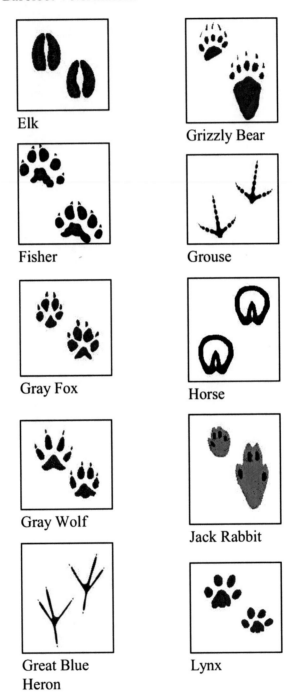

Elk

Grizzly Bear

Fisher

Grouse

Gray Fox

Horse

Gray Wolf

Jack Rabbit

Great Blue
Heron

Lynx

Mink

Mountain
Goat

Mountain
Lion

Mule Deer

Opossum

Raccoon

River Otter

Skunk

Muskrat

Wild Hog

Wolverine

Human
(or Barefoot
Veterinarian)

About the Authors

Lorrie Boldrick, D.V.M.

lives in Orange County, California with her two dogs, Tryin (Bernese Mountain Dog), and Seamus (Border Terrier) and her cat, Sarabi (Abyssinian). While much smaller than the menagerie she maintained for years, her current brood is much more manageable for pet-sitters when she engages in her favorite pastime - travel.

Her love of the exotic is not restricted to animals, as her travel destinations have included Machu Picchu, Antarctica, Australia, Africa, Madagascar, Costa Rica and Belize, among many others. She still spends plenty of time with the dogs and cats, though, as after a failed retirement, she reopened Quillie Acres Veterinary Clinic in 2003.

When not treating animals or exploring the globe, Lorrie enjoys walking with her dogs, bicycling with friends, reading and stained glass. Lorrie has also published four veterinary books – *Pygmy Goats Management and Veterinary Care, The Illustrated Standard of the Pygmy Goat, Pot-Bellied Pet Pigs Mini-Pig Care and Training* and *Veterinary Care of Pot-Bellied Pet Pigs.*

Michael Boldrick, Ph.D.

known as "Uncle Mike" or "Mikey" in several of the stories, is not a "real" doctor (i.e., a veterinarian ... or even an M.D.), but a Ph.D. engineer. Besides being a great co-author (especially if you prod him enough and take away his iPod), he is spearheading the development and implementation of world-class medical software. Mikey lives and travels with his best friend, Bashan, a twelve-year-old black Labrador Retriever. He loves the outdoors, especially the ocean, and often escapes from behind the keyboard to pursue his passion for triathlon.

Made in the USA